# THE PRETTIEST HOUSE ON THE BLOCK

## A REVEALING STORY OF DOMESTIC PARTNER ABUSE

Patricia A. Schoch

Blue Heron Book Works, LLC
Allentown, Pennsylvania

ISBN: 978-0-9991460-9-5
https://wordpress.com/view/patricschrn.wordpress.com
https://www.facebook.com/PatSchochAuthor/
Cover design by Angie Zambrano
Blue Heron Book Works, LLC
Allentown, Pennsylvania 18104
www.blueheronbookworks.com

# A Guy's Guy

The prettiest house on the block

He was such a nice guy

Silence is not always golden

Surviving his love

No more

*"Donna Miflin"*

# Table of Contents

*This book is dedicated to all survivors of Intimate Partner Violence and in memory of those who lost the fight.*

# ACKNOWLEDGMENTS

I would like to thank my family for putting up with me and my constant updates on the book, especially my husband, Denny, who had to live with it, and who picked up some of the slack while I was writing this story. You are all the best. I would especially like to thank "Donna Miflin" for opening up her life to me, allowing old wounds to reopen and become raw once again. That took courage and she came through, just as she did in overcoming her struggles in life. Thank you, "Donna."

# Introduction

Despite our age of enlightenment and the empowerment of women it showcases, intimate partner violence (IPV) and sexual assaults (SA) remain a tenacious problem in our country and in the world at large. In the United States, one in four women and one in ten men[1] will experience IPV in a lifetime, and these are just the cases that have been reported. We never hear from the silent sufferers. Whether overtly expressed or not, prevailing societal attitudes still seem to dictate that men are stronger and should be in control of women. The idea that women are supposed to be the weaker sex and subservient to men dates to biblical times and has somehow persisted through the ages. Although I believe that men of this generation are more sensitive to a woman's place in society and in the home than past generations, some of these patterns of behavior refuse to die, and until they do, we must be vigilant in our communication and education to both men and women.

For the purposes of this book only, victims will be referred to as women and abusers will be referred to as men because this is true in more cases than not and also because my subject is a woman. I do not mean to minimize men as victims, however, because they can be, and are. In fact, there are likely more cases than we know of because men often do not report their abuse. It is also written in this way for simplicity's sake. Make no mistake, though, men are at risk for abuse, also.

We can know the statistics and shake our heads in pity, and we can give someone all the resources at our fingertips to help them, but it's vital to remember that unless a victim understands why she enters into these relationships, it may be very difficult for her to change and she may find herself repeatedly being drawn to abusive men. In reading over my work, Donna, my subject, mentioned to me that she wishes she would have had the insights I talk about a long time ago. It was hard for her to see her life typed out on a Dell. The questions are, then, how does a woman become a victim of abuse, and how does the abuser become who he is? More importantly, how could Donna have shed the mindset that would allow the abuse that plagued her? Men are not born abusers, and women are not born victims. We are all born with our own unique palette of DNA, but nature alone does not create a person. Nurture picks up where nature leaves off. From the day we are born we are exposed to a multitude of influences collectively called nurture. Nature and nurture work together to form the kind of people we become as adults. This book will wade into the nature vs nurture debate and, hopefully, give you some tools to work with to overcome negative influences that may be subconsciously sabotaging your life.

For full disclosure, I am not a medical doctor, psychiatrist, or mental health worker; I am a Registered Nurse. None of the material in this book should be construed as professional advice; it is provided only as information relative to one person's story and to suggest ways for you to find help should you need it.

I have had a keen interest in mental health since my nursing school days, although I never worked in the field itself. I retired from full time nursing in 2015 after having spent 46 years in the profession. During that time, I had practiced in several different nursing disciplines in Bethlehem, Pennsylvania and Durham, Raleigh, Cary, Chapel Hill, and Rocky Mount, all in North Carolina. While working at Nash General in Rocky Mount, my head nurse approached me one day and said, "How would you like to learn how to put away bad guys?" This intrigued me, and I certainly did want to "put away" bad guys, so I readily agreed, without knowing exactly what I was getting myself into, but the intense course I was about to take spawned my interest in Forensic Nursing. Our class was the first of its kind in North Carolina and we initially called ourselves FNEs, or Forensic Nurse Examiners, but we were also known as SANEs, or Sexual Assault Nurse Examiners. We learned how to collect evidence for law enforcement from victims of sexual assault, domestic violence, and child abuse cases, the latter of which made my heart ache and my stomach turn. In the rare cases that ultimately made it to trial, we were called to be expert witnesses in the courtroom.

While still practicing as a nurse on a part time basis, I started doing freelance writing. Writing had been a dream for me for many years until I finally had the opportunity to pursue it. I had written two children's books that were published; I was maintaining a blog on WordPress; and I was doing freelance writing work when the opportunity to write this book came along. I had been writing for an online newspaper in Canada, the *Agora Cosmopolitan*. It's an edgy newspaper, and they liked controversial topics. Since I was writing health articles for them, I decided to write about two subjects I was passionate about: sexual assault and domestic violence. One article turned into four and I then published them on my blog as well. After I wrote the series and looked at the responses the articles garnered, I decided to write a book, an anthology of real stories about abused women and men, and I solicited cases. At first, I didn't get any takers—secrecy and shame are hallmarks of abuse—but one day I received a message from Donna asking, "Will you tell my story?" I recognized her name from a case I had been on more than a decade earlier, but she didn't immediately recognize my name until I told her who I was. You will learn what the connection was later. We knew immediately this partnership was meant to be. Obviously, I agreed, and after meeting with her the first time, I decided to tell only her story as the basis for a book to help her and others who may feel trapped in an unhealthy or dangerous relationship. The information on Donna and her experiences has been gleaned from personal interviews with her, sometimes at a trendy little coffee shop and sometimes at her home; entries from her journal; and entries from her husband, Max's, journal. She has given me complete access to these journals and permission to use any or all of this intimate information, providing that all names would be changed, which they have been.

I used my almost 50 years of experience in the medical field and much research to write this book. A physician and friend, Robert Hill MD, reviewed my book for medical accuracy, and my daughter-in-law, Kelly Schoch, a Genetic Counselor at Duke University in Durham, North Carolina, reviewed the information on genetics for accuracy. Thank you so much Rob and Kelly. I also feel very honored and grateful to Donna for opening her life to me, thus giving me the opportunity to combine my love of nursing, my love of writing, and my desire to help people to provide awareness and education for this ongoing blight on society.

Not all victims will live to tell their tragic tales, but fortunately, Donna Miflin did, and she wants to tell hers. No matter how many stories there are about abused women, they are like snowflakes, none are exactly alike. But there are commonalities and that's one of the things I want to emphasize in this book. I aim to offer solace to those who are in a dangerous situation and encouragement to those who are trying to escape but find it difficult, which it is. I want to offer hope to my readers that there are ways out for some women. I'm hoping that the information in this book gives you the knowledge and the courage to make the changes that you need to gain the happiness you deserve.

This book highlights the events of Donna's life and takes a look into the whys and wherefores of the behaviors that led to her situations, because she is not alone in them. If you see yourself, then this book is about you, too. It's a woman's personal story; it's about creating awareness of a troubling problem in society; it teaches about the factors that contribute to unhealthy patterns of behavior; and it contains information about emotional and medical issues that some of the characters in the book have suffered, which are part of the total portrait.

As you might expect, Donna Miflin is not her real name, nor are any of the other names in the book the same as the real people in her life. The story takes place in cities in New Jersey and North Carolina between 1953 and 2007.

All the situations in the book are real, but dialogue has been added and the details have been embellished for literary purposes. Embellishment aside, each one of these things did happen to Donna and scenarios have been created around events as they were told to me.

Hopefully, you will read this book cover to cover, but if you don't get past the introduction, please know that there is help for you, whether you are a victim or an abuser. You can change your life to find happiness, but you cannot do it alone; no one can. The painful truth is that not all women are able to break free of these chains, but my hope is that you will find a way, and that this book will help you in your quest for freedom. Usually, situations such as

Donna's start out well and deteriorate, but if you or someone you love has had a sudden change in behavior, becoming aggressive when he or she was not before, please schedule a medical evaluation to rule out a physical reason for the change. It may be due to a change in a person's feelings or to other life stressors, but please rule out illness first, for everyone's sake.

# Chapter 1

Seeds Are Planted

It was a perfect evening, Donna daydreamed, as the waiter at her favorite Italian restaurant took their orders. She had even been able to carve out some time in the day to have her hair and nails done before dinner. She chose a nail color to complement the new dress from Saks she had just purchased. It seemed there just weren't enough hours in the day to run her cosmetics business, get to the gym, and run the kids around to their multiple activities. They were so talented that she and her husband, Max, just couldn't deny them the chance to be the best they could be, and they were. Of course, that required even more time to rush around to special lessons, team practices, competitions, and concerts. That night was special because it was her birthday, her husband was home from his business trip, and the kids had all agreed to give up one night for the celebration. The four of them had even agreed to dig out their khaki's and clean, neatly ironed polo shirts for the occasion. Donna watched Max as he sipped his Dom Perignon. He looked around the table at his beautiful family, especially her. Her perfect manicure. Not a single hair out of place. And that sexy dress. Her workouts in the gym were paying off. Donna knew he was so proud of her: his beautiful, impeccably arranged wife and the four well-behaved children. She caught him looking at her and smiled as their eyes locked. She was proud of him as well. Successful businessman, smart, funny, considerate, and not at all hard on the eyes.

"I said something to you, Bitch!"

"What!" Startled, Donna managed to get out the word as Max's sharp admonition pierced the bubble in which her fantasy family was encased. "What did I do?" Donna wondered. Her mind rapidly scanned everything she could think of that would have raised his ire. "Did I leave the wrong clothes out for him or order the wrong drink for him?"

"You really are stupid, you know. I told you I don't like Italian."

Max's words stung as she could feel the blood slowly creeping up her face, flushing it with embarrassment as she tried to suppress the tears forming in her eyes.

Their son, Alex, shifted uncomfortably in his chair, looking down to avoid the probing eyes of the other customers. He was grateful when his phone rang, and he had an excuse to walk away from the table.

Donna's fantasy family faded away and she was forced back

into the fire of reality. *This* was her reality, not that perfect family she had created for herself, but why couldn't it be like that for her?

"I'm sorry," she apologized.

Max's biting words took her back to painful memories of abuse, alcohol, and drugs. His cruel words felt inexplicably comfortable to her, despite their emotional sting.

What is it that draws women to men that hurt them? For Donna Miflin, it was an extension of her childhood insecurity. She had been a sensitive child, a loner, never thinking she was good enough for anyone or anything. She often took the blame for things for which she was not at fault, imbedding unfounded guilt in her mind. Now, as an adult eating dinner at a fine restaurant, she was, once again, taking responsibility for what she considered to be a failure on her part. "Had he told me before that he didn't like Italian food, or did he make that up because there was nothing else for him to criticize?" she wondered. She even wondered if maybe she did know but did it as revenge for the daily verbal abuse that she received from him. If the latter was the motive for her choice in restaurants, then she knew it would incite his ire and she would pay for it with more cruelty. With all the guilt she carried around, it's possible that she believed she deserved his verbal abuse.

Donna was a product of an Italian family that had emigrated to the United States in the 1940's, escaping the political unrest in their country at that time and in search of a better life in America. Immigrants' hearts overflowed as Ellis Island and the Statue of

Liberty came into view, welcoming them and inviting their dreams. Her mother, Gina Di Orio, had been full of anticipation, excitement, and hope. She was about to bear her first child, and her husband, Mario, had gone on ahead to pave the way for their new lives. Gina's parents, Gino and Stephania DiOrio, and Mario's parents, Michael and Anna Perna, came along, also, as was common for European immigrant families. Gino and Stephania were executive chefs and were excited about establishing a nice Italian restaurant in America. Donna remembers being told that shortly after her family arrived in New York City, Donna's sister, Julianna, was born, and they made New York their home.

After ten years, however, Gina and Mario began to get discouraged with the way the city was becoming more crowded and busier and decided to move away, hoping they could give their family a better life elsewhere. Mario's parents opted to remain in New York City, but Mario, Gina, and her parents settled in Mahwah, a small town in New Jersey that sported a much different landscape than New York City. They found a cute colonial style home in a middle-class neighborhood with well-maintained properties and shade trees lining the streets. Moms chatted while their children played games on the sidewalk or rode bikes. It was only a short walk to a little downtown shopping area where people would go to buy, browse, or socialize, and they could walk to schools and churches. Mario's parents had come along temporarily to help Gina, Mario, Stephania and Gino set up their new house before the anticipated arrival of their second child, a baby girl, Donna. Stephania and Gino found the perfect building not far from their home to open a high-end Italian restaurant. Grandfather Gino took the late shift and cared for the girls during the day. Meanwhile, Gina found a job in a downtown jewelry store, and Mario found employment as a truck driver. But despite this good start, problems surfaced. Being a trucker, Mario was often absent, and, unfortunately, when he was not working, his constant companion was a bottle, either at home or at a local bar. Gina was absent, too, emotionally, and she and her daughters were not close.

From all outward appearances, the Perna and Di Orio families lived a peaceful, comfortable, life. However, an appealing exterior is not always painted from the same palette as are the lives inside the walls. Destructive entities such as alcoholism, drugs, and abuse, both emotional and physical, can lurk in any home. They're undeniable, undesirable commonalities that connect people, regardless of their stations in life.

Moving, itself, is a major life stressor, but moving from a new country with a different language must have been overwhelming. Somewhere, on their journey to the American Dream, the dream died, and Gina was left with an alcoholic husband and two young girls. That must have been when the barbed weeds began to wind their way up and around Gina, forbidding anyone to dare to get close to her and strangling out whatever hope of happiness she had left. She had to work, and, by this time, she could barely muster up enough courage and energy to go to work and care for herself, let alone her family. When speaking of her mother, Donna sadly describes her as having an "emotionless soul" with eyes that were unable to form tears, tears that must have been cascading around her heart like a cold waterfall. How can a woman take care of other souls when hers lives in a void? Gina did have her parents to help her, although I'm not sure how much help "an old Italian bitch," as Donna describes her grandmother, was in raising two young girls. Luckily, Donna's grandfather was a different story. Gino adored the girls and was not afraid to show them.

"Hey, Donna. Come here to Nonno," her grandfather would say, and she would eagerly scramble up on his lap and bury herself in his arms, breathing in deeply the comforting aroma of Italian food that had permanently imbedded itself in his clothing.

"What do you want for supper?" he asked with a big smile for his youngest granddaughter.

"Spaghetti!" she yelled.

"Again?!" Gino teased her.

"Yes, again!" Donna giggled.

Gino's face lit up and his dark eyes sparkled whenever he saw Donna, and she melted in the warmth of his gaze. Everyone always seemed to be too busy for the girls, but not their Nonno. With him, Donna felt safe, loved, and secure. He was her rock, her security, and her cushion, all rolled into one. They played games and he would always let her win. He watched her color pictures in a coloring book, and sometimes even colored with her. She loved to draw him pictures with hearts and flowers all over the page, and he smiled at his special gifts. Sometimes she thought that she saw tears forming in his eyes, but he would deny it.

"Dust," he said.

He told her stories of Old Italy, and she came to know her roots. He meant everything to her, and she to him. She was happy when she was with her Nonno, and time stood still, all the way up until the day it really did stand still for Donna.

"Gina!" she heard an anguished voice calling her mother.

Donna ran after Gina towards the sound of her grandfather's voice and looked on in horror as she saw her Nonno on the kitchen floor, struggling to breathe, clutching his chest, perspiration dripping from his face and his color draining away, antacid tablets strewn across the floor where he lay.

"Call an ambulance," he directed Gina, his breathing becoming more labored and his voice weaker.

After what seemed like an eternity, she heard the ominous wail of ambulance sirens getting louder as they approached her home. She felt like a stake was being shoved right through her heart as she watched the emergency responders race up the street, deftly avoiding the cars parked on both sides. The gurney bumped around as it was guided up the front steps into the kitchen, where her Nonno was trying to talk.

"I thought it was just heartburn," he whispered, "but the antacids didn't help."

In her state of shock, Donna could barely discern what the emergency responders were doing. At that time, emergency responders ran on a "scoop and run" system. They were not even trained in CPR back then. They just hurriedly loaded patients onto a stretcher and transported them to the nearest hospital. As they prepared to push him out into the ambulance, Gino looked over at his family, who were by his side throughout this whole ordeal, and whispered in a raspy voice, "Don't worry about me. I'll be alright. I love you."

He smiled at them, took a rattling-sounding deep breath and closed his eyes. His chest was still. He didn't respond to his family's pleas to not leave them.

Donna watched in terrified shock as life gradually ebbed away from her beloved Nonno's body. Her rock had crumbled into a thousand pieces right before her eyes. Her companion, the source of the only love she felt, her only sense of security, was lost to her at the tender age of six years old, and before she could even say goodbye. She remembers nothing after that until the priest arrived after Gino's death to administer the Last Rites of the Roman Catholic Church.

# Chapter 2

Daddy Dearest

Donna was devastated and felt forever lost after that, desperately grasping at only a memory of the love that could no longer be returned, or ever duplicated. Her grandfather's death was the beginning of a lifetime of insecurity, guilt, and isolation that Donna could never seem to shake, a life that she would later describe as one defined by loss and loneliness. The grief over the loss of her Nonno was unbearable, and she would have given anything in her young life to have him back. She had recurring nightmares about him and his death for a long time afterward. Donna was alone much of the time after that, even when she was sick, which was often. Physically, she was a thin, fragile child, frequently ill with fevers, anemia, infections, and joint pain, without anyone understanding why. Hindsight being 20/20, she wonders if this was just a foretaste of the Lupus Erythematosus that would be diagnosed later in life.

Emotionally, she was insecure, nervous, and socially awkward, never thinking she was good enough for anyone or that she could do anything right. Her role models at home were either mean, unhappy, emotionally absent, or drunk. Donna had no blueprint for a happy life. Mario was home sometimes, but when he was, he was usually drunk. She knows her parents had fights, but Donna doesn't remember the actual incidents. Maybe Mario waited until Donna was in bed to smack her mom around, or maybe she has repressed the memories of the fights. She does, however, remember her mother's bruises and the black eyes that looked like some sort of macabre face art, attracting interest from others and inspiring questions that usually remained unasked. These remnants of physical arguments allegedly stemming from events such as a "car accident," to cite one explanation, served as a keen reminder of the dysfunctional family of which she was a part. She was frightened, but her daddy never hurt her or her sister, only her mother.

Repression is a merciful function of the brain that helps to prevent traumatic memories from intruding on our consciousness. Thankfully, it seems Donna was able to use this defense mechanism to deal with some of the pain inflicted on her in her conscious world.

Donna recalls she and her dad going for "rides", but she always knew where the car was headed. Mario couldn't care for his children even when the burden of responsibility for their well-being fell squarely on his shoulders. One evening, Mario pulled up in front of his favorite hang-out, opened his own door and got out.

"Stay in the car, Donna, and lock the doors. Daddy is stopping here for a few minutes. I'll be right back."

Donna watched as Mario entered the bar, avoiding a stumbling, disheveled bar patron on his way out. The sad-looking man shuffled down the street, pausing only long enough to vomit in a yew bush. Donna knew that "right back" had a very flexible definition for Mario, so she passed the time counting cars and daydreaming, or more accurately, late evening dreaming. Eventually, the traffic slowed down, and she got bored. There is only so much an active youngster can do alone in the back seat of a car. Disobeying Mario's instructions, Donna got out of the car and timidly made her way up the steps and into the dingy bar.

"Hey, Mario. I think you have company," said the bartender as Donna walked through the door amidst stares. He was a "regular," and by now, she was, too.

"Maybe you'd better take her and head home."

"Nah, she's fine. Just give her a Shirley Temple," said Mario, as he plopped her up on the worn, swiveling barstool next to him and went back to his own drink. Donna liked Shirley Temples, the non-alcoholic beverages named after the cute and innocent child actress with her distinctive blonde curls. But she didn't like the "dark and smoky bar with its funky smell, like beer when it ferments" which was, in fact, exactly what the smell was. She closed her eyes and tried to call up the tantalizing aroma that emanated from the German bakery just down the street, where they got rolls and a two-layer chocolate cake every Sunday after church, but the funky smell of the bar was too overwhelming to allow the virtual warm smell of goodness to break through the smoky stench. She waited uncomfortably while her Daddy drank enough of his poison to numb his sensibilities enough to face life outside of the bar, or until his money ran out, whichever came first. Donna was an observant child, and she noticed the bartender pick up the phone, glance furtively at her father, then dial a number.

"Hey, Gina," Donna heard the bartender say. "I think you should come get your old man and the kid. I don't think he should be drivin' home." After a brief pause, she heard the voice on the phone say, "Yeah. I'll get 'em."

Relieved that her mom was coming to get them out of there, Donna relaxed after she saw the man grab Mario's car keys off the bar counter. He had never even bothered to put them away before he started drinking and was oblivious to the fact that they were no longer there.

"What are *you* doing here?!" Mario slurred at the sight of his wife coming through the door.

"Come on, we're going home," Gina said in disgust.

Taking Donna's one hand, Gina supported Mario with her other one as he stumbled out of the bar and into her car. He was out cold before she even got the car started. Even at her young age, Donna wondered why her mom put up with this man. Gina knew that he drank, smoked, gambled, and ran around on her. When he ran out of money, he would steal the furs and jewelry he had given her as peace offerings for his misdeeds and sell them to support his indulgences. There was just something about that "bad boy" persona to which some women are drawn. Her dad was handsome, fun and could be quite charming. It was understandable that he would be able to find another woman when one didn't work out for him.

Donna isn't exactly sure when it happened, but the next thing she remembers, he was gone. She was blessed, or cursed, with a detailed recall system for the events in her life, but many memories of life with her father after he left them are gone. When he walked out on them, her brain went into the survival mode of repression to protect her from conjuring up any more pain than she was already feeling from the loss. Some people might say "What loss?" He was an often absent, mostly inattentive, abusive, alcohol-addicted man, and yet, a loss of even a negative thing is still a loss, and a disruption in Donna's life, dysfunctional as it was. It may not have been as much associated with the physical loss, but more a symbol of the loss of the father she wanted and deserved to have had. Can you imagine what she was thinking when he left? "What did I do wrong? Was I bad? Is it my fault he left? Will Mommy blame me?" She didn't need one more thing to stick up on her Guilt Board. It was already covered with enough virtual guilt post-it notes. She later learned her daddy had skipped town with his lady-friend and relocated to Jersey City, effectively ejecting himself from the life he had and the people who depended on him. He and his new love, Mary, were hardy partiers in the drug and alcohol scene in New Jersey, and Donna suspects the Other Woman didn't care much about the person he really was as much as what she could get out of the relationship. Oddly, her mother, Gina, never cried. Perhaps that was her way of coping, but if she was hurt by the loss, she never showed it. Bereft of emotion, Gina went on about her business, never looking back. Donna recalls the time that she was home sick, alone again, when someone knocked on the door.

"Donna are you there?" a woman said through the door. But Donna didn't recognize her voice, so she didn't answer. Even though she was home alone often, she couldn't help but be frightened of someone she didn't know at the door.

"Donna it's your dad's friend, Mary. He said it was ok to come and talk to you."

Donna still didn't answer.

"I just want to meet you and talk with you for a while. I'd like to get to know you. May I come in?"

Donna quickly called her mom at work. But by the time Gina arrived, Mary was gone.

"You did the right thing, Donna," said Gina.

Donna's fear dissolved now that her mom was with her. That had the potential of being a very bad situation for a child left alone, but this time danger took a bye. It wasn't a stranger there to do her harm, but Mario's girlfriend. Still, small, thin Donna wondered what she would do if a real bad guy showed up at the door and broke in.

Mario had made his choice, and Gina filed for divorce. After the divorce he was granted visitation rights and the vaults in Donna's memory bank gradually and cautiously unlocked. She fondly remembers him bringing her gifts: a big doll, a toy ice-skating rink, snails in a paper bag, and large purple gumballs in a tube. He taught her how to play Craps and she still has his dice, but she paid a high price for these memories, watching her father waste his life. Alcohol is a cunning mistress and no number of gifts could disguise the devastation or wipe away the ever-growing resentment she caused. Her father's visits diminished as Donna grew older, and with them, her interest in ever even seeing her father again. Resentment grew as a child's innocence was replaced by the more tensile awareness of a teenager regarding some of the negative influences her father's presence and betrayal had on her and her sister. This resentment surged the day 13-year old Donna took a phone call from her father.

"Hello?" Donna answered the phone with a business-as-usual attitude.

"Donna, it's Daddy."

Donna's facial muscles tightened, and her jaws clenched.

"What do you want? I'm busy." Donna answered tersely.

"I want you to come and see me. I'm in the hospital for some tests and I want to talk to you," Mario said.

Conflicting emotions battled for control. Donna regained her composure before she answered him. "I'm sorry that you are sick, but I don't want to talk to you," she finally managed to spit out.

"Please, Donna. I really need to talk to you. I'm sorry for everything I have done," Mario said, apologetically.

"Maybe later," Donna said, trying to end the conversation without sounding as harsh as she felt inside. "I really am busy right now. I have a lot of homework to do," she said, grateful for an excuse to answer honestly.

"Okay, so maybe I'll see you later, then?" he asked.

"Maybe. I'll see. Good night, Dad."

"Good night, Donna." He waited until he heard the click on the other end of the line before he hung up, hoping Donna might change her mind and talk to him.

Donna was grateful Gina didn't force her to either speak to her father or visit him. She was 13 years old now, too old, she thought, to be forced to visit someone she wanted nothing to do with. She absentmindedly finished her homework that night and went to school as usual the next day, but her mind wasn't on her classes; it was on the last night's conversation with her father. Did she do the right thing, or was she just being selfish?

After school, she and her friend, Joe Russo, who lived next-door, went in Joe's house, where the smell of his mother's brownies met them as they opened the door. Donna often went to the Russo's house when no one was at her house. She liked Joe and his mom, and they were good company, much better than being home alone.

She envied Joe's close-knit family. Sometimes she would fantasize her mother being at their home when she got home from school, warm brownies awaiting her. Gina would be in the kitchen taking them out of the oven and starting to make supper for her hard-working husband. She would greet Donna with a smile and a hug, and Donna would help set the table for dinner. The smell of brownies would soon be replaced by the tantalizing aroma of spicy lasagna. Around 5:30 PM Mario would come home, tired from his long day but eager to see his family. A chilled glass of water awaited him because he no longer drank alcohol. He had stopped driving trucks and gotten a job as a construction worker, so he wasn't gone as much. His olive skin was even darker now, tanned from working in the sun, and Gina and Mario loved each other dearly.

Then Donna would sigh and come back to reality, fantasy over.

"Hi, Mrs. Russo!" said Donna.

"Hi, Donna. Hi, Joe," replied Mrs. Russo. "How was your day?"

"Fine," they said in unison.

Mrs. Russo smiled at their predictable answer. "Fine" was the standard teenage answer to that question. Sometimes she was lucky enough to hear about it later in the evening. What are you two up to, today?" she asked.

"We're going to work on this geography project," said Donna.

"How do we do a topography of the United States? What IS a topography?" Joe asked.

Donna laughed. "We'll figure it out."

Joe wrinkled his nose up in displeasure at the thought of doing homework but followed Donna's lead. They headed down to the basement where they could spread all their supplies out and work.

The sharp ring of the phone pierced the quiet house and they both jumped. In a minute, Mrs. Russo came downstairs.

"Donna, that was your mom," said Mrs. Russo. "Your Dad has had a stroke and he is asking to see you. She said you can't say 'no' this time. She and Julianna are coming to pick you up to go to the hospital."

A thousand thoughts and feelings swam around in her head. "Okay," she said, trying to identify her emotions.

What *was* she feeling? She didn't know if it was love, hate, fear, guilt, sorrow, pity, or all of them. She recalled a conversation between Mario's doctor and her mom one day.

"Gina, you have to get Mario to stop drinking and smoking or those things will kill him before his time," he warned.

"I know," her mom said, "but I can't help him if he doesn't want help. If I try to throw his cigarettes away, or dump his bottles of booze, he gets furious and I'm terrified that he will hurt me or the girls. I'll try, but I don't think there is anything I can do."

"Did his habits finally catch up with him," Donna wondered. "Was it 'his time'?"

"I'm sorry about your dad, Donna," Joe said. "I'll work on this by myself for now. I hope he's okay."

She nodded her acknowledgement of his sentiments, never looking up from the floor, and they put their project aside. Donna went home and went through the motions of getting ready for a visit with her ill, estranged father in the hospital, those mixed feelings tearing around her heart like racing cars vying for First Place at the finish line. Then she turned on the TV and fell onto the couch to pass the time and collect her thoughts. A short time later she heard the door open and close. Gina and Julianna had arrived to pick her up. The two went up to their bedrooms to get a few things, but before they could leave, another insistent ringing of the phone startled

Donna once again. A brief silence was followed by a bloodcurdling scream from upstairs. Donna froze. Julianna was crying hysterically. Terrified, she turned around to go upstairs and immediately felt an inexplicable peace passing through her. Sensing another presence in the room, she looked up, her eyes meeting a bright white image. Somehow, she knew immediately that it was an angel, and she was no longer afraid. The angel brought her a comfort she had never felt before, and delivered this gentle message: "Don't be scared, Donna. Your father has died but everything will be okay."

If Donna had ever wondered where her father would be in the afterlife, she no longer did. She knew he would be alright. Mario believed in God, and even though she was having trouble forgiving him, she knew that God would. The angel just clarified something of which she would not have been sure, otherwise. One thing she didn't need an angel to tell her, though, was that her father was gone.

Donna Miflin may not have been abused all her life, but childhood experiences, both seen and heard, served to weave an intricate pattern of self-destruction into a dark cloak that would cover her for almost her entire life. The permeable fibers of this cloak made her open to the control of others, especially men. It did not allow her to say "no," even when she wanted to or knew she should. It prevented the emergence of any semblance of self-esteem, which may have empowered her to make better choices in her life. When such a dark cloak is created early in life as was Donna's, it can be extremely tricky to shed. Dirt gets imbedded in the weave, and unless a means of cleansing the cloak presents itself, it gets heavier to bear. Mario's death just added another dark strand to the cloak. It had hurt when she heard how he talked to her mother and when she saw the bruises on Gina's face. It hurt when she saw him drink himself into oblivion. It hurt when he ignored her even when he was with her. It hurt that he left her, Julianna, and Gina alone to run off with another woman, and maybe some might think it shouldn't have, but it still hurt when he died. Along with the bad memories, the good ones began to surface in her memory banks, as well as the question of what she could have done better. Even though he caused more pain than joy for Donna, his death was a loss for her.

# Chapter 3

Coping with Loss

Donna's angel had delivered a message of peace about her father, but the peace she felt was short-lived. She was wracked with guilt for not going to him when he asked her. She never forgave herself for not forgiving him, not saying goodbye, and it cast an aura of darkness over her for years. It's been said that offering forgiveness to someone is as good for the forgiver as the person being forgiven, but Donna fell short of earning that happy ending. She was numb. The smell of death haunted her, not in the form of an unpleasant olfactory presence, but in the form of beautiful lilies, like the ones at her dad's funeral that were supposed to brighten up the dark day. The fragrant flowers that adorn gardens and vases, bringing smiles to faces, are now, for Donna, a stinging reminder of death, regret and failure. She wondered if she would ever be the same, if anyone would ever love her, take care of her. Once again, she was lost and alone, left with only a cold mother and an uncontrolled sister, neither of whom were sources of comfort.

With the sudden loss of her father came the stark realization that, not only had she just lost her dad, but she had lost something she never really had to begin with, and now could never gain. Donna knew that Mario loved her, but she had never experienced that undying love of a daddy who was there for her through thick and thin, who worshipped her and stood up for her if she was wronged. She never had a daddy who called her his little Princess or read her bedtime stories. And now, for better or for worse, she had no daddy at all. No one to guide her through life. No one to walk her down the aisle and kiss her gently while placing her hand in the hand of her Prince Charming. What was she mourning, the loss of her father or the loss of what could have been but never was, and never can be?

It's odd how we can mourn the loss of someone whose presence in our lives was nothing but a source of pain. Good or bad, the people we lose used to be in our lives, and now they're gone.

Domestic violence associates itself with this dynamic. Leaving an abuser is unquestionably the best thing for a victim, but that would mean that there would be a loss suffered. Painful as the situation might be, it still means that a piece of someone's life will go missing. Divorce or even toxic friendships can cause these dichotomous feelings, as well. The love or affection may be gone, but what two people have shared is a chapter in their book of life. The end of the relationship still hurts, and when there is guilt involved, such as from not responding to a death bed request from one's source of pain, the emotional load can be unbearable, as it was for Donna.

However, having an explanation for these choices for remaining with someone who is hurting you should not be confused with having a reason. There are counselors and other mental health providers who can help you sort out and work through whatever is preventing you from attaining the freedom that you desire and require. Don't ever think you are the only one with baggage, because you aren't. We all have it in varying degrees and amounts, and everyone is dealing with something. You are not alone.

Donna's sister, Julianna, dealt with the impact of their losses in her own way. While Donna was feeling guilt and pain, Julianna's predominant emotion was deep anger at the circumstances of her life. There were ten years difference between Donna and Julianna, so they were never quite in sync with each other's stage of life. After their grandfather died, they were left alone the larger part of their lives. Everyone else was still alive when Mario died, but no one was home during the day at all, which suited teenager Julianna just fine.

"Donna, can't you go do something?" Julianna would ask, as what seemed like a parade of boys came and went to visit. "If you must be in the house, go to another room and keep your mouth shut." Julianna resented having to tend to her little sister when she had company.

"I wish Nonno was still here," Donna said, tearfully. "He wouldn't let you do this. You're going to get in trouble."

"Well, he isn't. No one else ever is, either, and no one cares," said Julianna, angrily, "so mind your own business and go do something else. No one will know unless YOU tell them, and you won't do that, will you?" The look on Julianna's face was not a happy one, and Donna shook her head. She wasn't going to cross her.

"Jules, where's the weed?" someone slurred, already wasted from an appetizer of booze.

"Shut up! I'll be there as soon as I deal with my nosy sister," Julianna said.

Julianna was out of control and there was no one there to supervise or guide her. They both were being adversely affected by their childhood lives and, at age 18, right after she graduated from high school, Julianna got pregnant. Her boyfriend did the honorable thing, though, and married her. Sadly, though, it would not turn out to be a match made in Heaven. Simon was a talented musician, the lead singer of his own band, and Julianna loved to go to his gigs and watch the band play before the baby came, but the marriage was fraught with physical and emotional abuse for her. She finally summoned up the courage to leave him and get a divorce, a brave step for an abused young woman, and moved back home with Gina and Donna, young son in tow, where she felt safe.

Donna and Julianna didn't know what love was or even how to identify healthy love should they find it, because neither one was provided with that blueprint.

Loss, with its attendant grief, can manifest itself in various emotions and can be different for each person. Where Donna dealt with her loss through sadness and guilt, and Julianna dealt with hers through anger, Gina, already withdrawn, now steeled herself and built walls. She threw herself into work, sacrificing a closeness with her girls that every mother and daughter should have. Working helped her to escape from her own pain but also caused that pain to be transferred to her daughters in the process. Sometimes what appears to be strength and stability, such as drowning oneself in work, can be a manifestation of a perpetual fear of facing the world and its more painful responsibilities, a prolonged period of disguised grief from loss. I'm sure there are layers to Gina about which I have no knowledge, but this is what Donna saw: an emotionless woman who never cried. Ignoring grief is not a healthy way to cope because it will surface and affect your life in some way at another time. I liken smothered pain to dirt in a stovepipe. There is just so much dirt and soot a pipe can hold, and if we keep creating more soot and pushing it down into the pipe over and over again, eventually it will spill out over the top, soiling the area around it. People must grieve their losses or express their feelings, no matter how long it takes or how they do it. If grief is what is holding you back from being free, or if you are afraid of experiencing a loss, find a good counselor to help you work it through. You can cry, because it's okay to cry. It can be good for you, and it isn't a sign of weakness. Don't judge someone if they don't cry over a loss, though. They may be dealing with it in ways you don't know.

Grief doesn't only show itself after the death of a loved one. It can occur after any loss: a pet, a divorce, losing a friendship, the loss of a job, or even the death of a dream. These can feel just as real as someone's death to the one who is suffering the loss. Working through grief is essential for people to move on with their lives, and although everyone grieves in their own ways, a process to do so was identified in 1969 by the late psychiatrist, Dr. Elizabeth Kubler Ross. She determined that there are five stages of grief: 1) Denial: "This is not happening." 2) Anger: "Why did this have to happen?" 3) Bargaining (with God): "Please make this not happen and I'll do_____." 4) Depression: "Just leave me alone; I'm too sad to think about anything or do anything," and finally 5) Acceptance: "I have accepted what's happened, and I'll be okay."

Not everyone goes through every stage and the stages don't necessarily occur in the same order, but the goal for everyone is to end up at stage 5: Acceptance.[2] Resolving your grief doesn't mean you will, or need to, forget your loved one. If you find yourself caught in one of these stages, know that it's all part of the natural process of healing, and please don't give up. Give yourself some space to heal; grief has no timetable. Just as everyone's personality is different, so are everyone's coping skills. Every loss is different, and every response to that loss is different. It can take months and even years to work through the pain and that's okay, if that's what it takes for you. Don't judge yourself harshly if it's not happening as fast as you think it should. Information on grief and loss abounds if you want to learn more, and I encourage that for anyone. Take advantage of support from friends, family, spiritual leaders, support groups, or a professional mental health provider, but don't try to go it alone, and don't ever give up. Remember that people have suffered losses since the dawn of humanity and have survived, and you can, too. You got this!

# Chapter 4

Actions, Consequences, and Decisions

Donna's teenage years are not a source of pride for her, but of shame. Just as her sister before her, Donna was "looking for love in all the wrong places" and "in too many faces," the words that have been immortalized in song by country singer Johnny Lee. Sadly, she didn't learn from Julianna's poor decisions, and she became promiscuous, desperately searching for acceptance and approval from the male gender. High school should be one of the right places to learn about love, or at least to practice the art of relationships, but the high school years can also serve to expose young people to the pain of heartbreak and to the truths and consequences of decision-making. Without guidance, these normal high school growing pains can be confusing and hard to manage. Donna dodged bullets aimed at her sexually promiscuous behavior for a while, but then she met Jimmy, a smooth-talking, handsome young man who had graduated from high school the year before, making him three years her senior, and they became a couple. What she got from that relationship is that abusive attention beats no attention, and thus began her journey into victimhood and survival.

Donna squirmed around in a chair, rehearsing multiple versions of what she would say to Jimmy that day. Maybe she wouldn't even tell him. No, he needed to know, but she had to tell him somewhere in a public, and yet still private, place. She didn't want the whole world to know but she wanted people around so he wouldn't hurt her when she told him. Donna was acutely aware that his response to anger was to push her, shove her, or smack her if she made him mad. She decided that a public park by the river would be a safe place to meet. Jimmy picked her up and they drove to the park, which was not too far from Donna's house. It was a beautiful day and they sat on a weathered park bench watching children play on the swings and jungle gym as the leaves on the trees waved to them. She squirmed around again, as if shifting in her seat would give her the courage that she needed to tell Jimmy her news.

"What's the matter with you today? You're so jumpy," Jimmy said as he watched her fidgeting.

"I don't know. I'm just extra nervous today or something," she lied.

"Well, there's something wrong with you. I know you're a nervous chick, but you're worse today," he said.

"I'm pregnant," the frightened high school sophomore finally blurted out, feeling dizzy from her heart pounding so hard and fast.

"You're what? You're pregnant? Are you sure? Maybe you're just a little late."

"No, Jimmy. Julianna took me to a doctor, and I'm definitely pregnant." She relaxed a little as she looked down at his unclenched fists.

"What are we going to do about it?" he asked.

"I don't know. I'll probably give the baby up for adoption," Donna said.

"Why don't we get married?" said Jimmy, almost a bit too quickly.

Donna was stunned. "I don't know if that would be a good idea. I still have two more years to go in high school."

This was true, and certainly enough to hide the real reasons she didn't want to marry Jimmy. She didn't love him, and she was wary of the pattern of abuse that had begun in their relationship. Donna was surprised, at first, that Jimmy was willing to do the right thing by her, but what came out of his mouth next explained his sudden interest in marriage, and not much of a shock to her, knowing Jimmy.

"I just got my draft number and it's low," said Jimmy. "I'll be going to Vietnam, but if I'm married, I won't have to go on active duty. We can live on the base at Fort Dix. I don't want to go over there and die in that place for no reason."

"Really, Jimmy? You want to get married just so you don't have to go to Vietnam?  I'm sorry. That's not a good reason to get married. We're just too young. I don't want to marry you right now," said Donna, feeling more confident.

"But why? You know I love you. That baby needs a father. You can finish high school there, and we can start our own family," said Jimmy.

Donna thought she had never seen him look so vulnerable before, but she resisted his self-serving pleading.

"I'm sorry. I just don't want to get married to you," maintained Donna. "Why would I want to marry someone who smacks me every time he doesn't get his way or doesn't like what I say or do? Maybe the baby would even be in danger."

"I won't ever hit you again, Donna, I swear. I don't know what gets into me, sometimes. I'll be different once I move away from my parents and in with you, and I would never hit a child," Jimmy said. He actually sounded sincere.

"That's what my father always said to my mother and what Simon said to Julianna, and you know how those worked out. No, I won't marry you."

Donna stood her ground and Jimmy finally gave up. It was obvious to her that he felt rejected, angry, and scared.

Jimmy jumped in his car and raced off, tires squealing.

Shaking and crying, Donna stayed on the park bench to compose herself before she went home to tell her mom. She wasn't looking forward to that.

Gina was furious.

"Donna, how could you let this happen, especially since your sister? You're only 15! If you had to have sex, why didn't you use protection? And now you tell me Jimmy wants to marry you, and you won't do it? How are you going to manage without a father for the baby? You haven't even finished high school, and John and I can't take care of a baby. That's not fair to either of us. You and Jimmy have to get married."

"Mom, I didn't plan on having sex. I didn't want to. I told Jimmy I wasn't ready, but he said he loved me and if I loved him, I would do it. I was afraid to make him mad. What would you have said if I had asked you to take me to the doctor for birth control pills? It just happened and I didn't think I would get pregnant. We only did it a few times."

"It only takes once," said Gina, "and it would be well for you to remember that from now on."

"Mom, Jimmy hits me. I can't have a baby with him, and I don't love him, either. Do you really want me to marry someone like that just to save face? We're only teenagers. We can't do this. Look what happened to Julianna and Simon. I'm going to have this baby and give it up for adoption to someone who really wants a child and can take care of it."

Gina had remarried by this time, and Donna liked her stepfather, John. She felt disappointed that she had let them down and she knew her mom was right; it wouldn't be fair to them, which is why she had already decided to give the baby up for adoption. Gina was tiring of the futility of trying to advise Donna. "Well, I guess you have to do what you have to do," she begrudgingly conceded.

At that time, the family had been preparing to move out of town.

The timing could not have been better, since now they could all be spared the embarrassment of having an unwed, pregnant teenager in a place where everyone knew them. They moved into an upscale neighborhood where Donna felt ill at ease. She never felt like she fit in anywhere, and that old self-esteem issue reared its ugly head once again in this new, upper-class environment.

Donna dropped out of school temporarily, carried her baby boy to full term, and reluctantly made plans to surrender him to his new parents. She had planned to give the baby up right from the start, but after you carry a baby in your womb for nine months your heart changes, and hers ached to see her baby boy. Sadly, all the nurses and doctors told her that "it would be best if she didn't see him."

Then Jean, a compassionate nurse that Donna had come to like, asked her, "Donna, do you want to see your baby?"

"Could you do that?" she asked, hopefully. "They told me I shouldn't see him or hold him."

"I'm not supposed to do it, but I won't tell anyone if you don't," Jean said with a smile and a wink. "I think you should be able to hold your own baby and say goodbye."

Nurse Jean managed to sneak the baby boy out of the nursery, and she placed him in his mother's waiting arms. Donna was blessed with one brief, beautiful moment with her son, and she gave him a kiss that would have to last a lifetime.

"I love you, baby boy. I'm doing what is best for you," said Donna through tears.

With tears in her own eyes, Jean gently took Baby Boy Di Orio from his mother's arms and returned him to the nursery. From there he would go home with new parents, people with an intact marriage, people who had the means to support him, people who were not teenagers. Donna would go on to raise three more boys after that, but she never stopped thinking about that baby boy, her first child. Jimmy did go to Vietnam, eventually returning in one piece, but he and Donna never reconnected.

The human brain is a complex thing, considering that the trauma of neglect, exposure to alcoholism, rejection, and loss can dwell there and drive the decisions we make later in life. Research shows that individuals who have experienced significant trauma in childhood are less able to adequately determine risks as youth and adults, leaving them open to dangers and failure that can add to already burdened hearts and minds.[3] Some studies show that traumatic childhoods rewire the brain, bypassing the area that is involved in healthy decision-making. It would certainly make sense, then, that up to 90 % of offenders in youth detention centers and jails have experienced significant trauma in their young lives.[4] What does this mean for crime and punishment? These ideas are already being used in courtrooms in attempts to dilute sentences. Will an attorney soon be able to say, "You can't convict this person. He is a victim, too. His childhood made him do it. Acquit!" Will judicial sentences continue to be gradually watered down, or even become non-existent? What effect would that have on law and order if criminals are allowed back on the streets with no consequences for their actions?

On the more positive end of research results, it has been suggested that training centers designed to teach the brain how to engage in better decision-making processes can reduce the chances that people with tendencies towards aberrant behavior will get in trouble. Some believe that the brain can be re-trained to better handle life's choices. Could this evolve into routine therapy for at-risk children and youth before trauma manifests itself in crime? What hopeful possibilities these studies represent to stem the tide of crime and misery.[5]

Considering the research, it's not surprising that survivors like Donna make poor decisions in life. Donna's childhood traumas had wound themselves together like a tight sailor's knot to create a nervous, insecure, needy child. Even her teachers had told her mother that she needed acceptance and constant reassurance of her worth. For Donna, the loneliness and insecurity in her childhood world led to a life of promiscuity, accidental pregnancy, drugs, and abuse by men in her adult world. If you are familiar with *Maslow's Hierarchy of Needs,* you may remember that love and belonging, safety, self-esteem, stability, freedom from fear, and positive intimate relationships are all building blocks in the construction of a healthy mind and body.[6] Maslow believed that if a house is missing a few of these blocks, a person cannot be completely whole and strong. It isn't hard, then, to understand how children who are deprived of one or more of these basic needs look elsewhere for need fulfillment as adults and can wind up making poor life choices.

These poor choices can hurt oneself, but when abusers make bad decisions, the pain trickles down to others. We can understand criminal behavior with knowledge of how difficult childhoods can affect brain functions and decision-making, and we can even feel pity for the perpetrators of crimes; but understanding that behavior and excusing it are two different things. Criminals certainly have rights, too, but behavior that violates the rights of others should never be excused without some sort of consequence being dealt.

Donna's lack of proper nurturing resulted in her inability to say no to Jimmy. She thought someone loved her, and she liked how that felt, even though she may not have loved him as much in return. She "gave in" to him, and although the sex may have been consensual in some eyes, it was not. It was a sexual assault. "No" means "no," and if a woman must be coerced into having sexual contact, then it is not consensual, it is coercion, especially if a woman complies due to fear of physical or emotional injury from her partner.

It's the responsibility of parents to make children feel loved and wanted so they don't look elsewhere for that need to be fulfilled.


Close your eyes. If you have had a good childhood, smile and give thanks. Now picture yourself as a child. Remove a parent, financial security, love, and or safety and security from your picture and try the best that you can to imagine how you might feel. It's hard, maybe impossible, isn't it? But if you were able to imagine an inkling of a feeling of fear, loneliness, pain, or insecurity, then you may have felt a drop in the turbulent pool of an abused person's life.

# Chapter 5

Not My Child

Donna finished high school after the baby was born and lived with her mother and stepfather until she met and married her first husband, Thomas Gardner, and they set up housekeeping in a place on his family's small farm in New Jersey. Donna and Tom had two boys during their marriage, George and Josh, but George was the one that put their patience, and their marriage, to the test. Although her husband was not physically abusive, he was emotionally vacant and cold, traits to which she had been accustomed all her life, so Donna, undoubtedly, didn't comprehend that this was not the way a marriage was supposed to be. She needed that missing blueprint for life.

Donna suspected from an early age that George was different. He wasn't like the other kids who played with each other and were capable of normal interactions. No, George stayed in the shadows, looking to the ground and kicking dirt around, anger brewing as

Donna tried to encourage him to play with the other boys. When his anger finally bubbled to the top it was like a fierce storm at sea, waves battling each other for control. All Donna could think to herself was, "Not my child…." This exemplifies the denial phase of loss or grief as discussed earlier, paraphrased: "This can't be happening to my child." Loss can be subtle sometimes. Donna was grieving the loss of her healthy son to one whose actions were unacceptable to her.

One night, when George was three years old and Donna was asleep in her bed, she was awakened by the sound of a chair moving on the floor downstairs in the kitchen. Figuring it was just Tom getting up for a snack, she rolled over and went back to sleep. Awakening the next morning, she headed for the kitchen to make coffee, but what greeted her made her heart skip a beat: sugar splayed out across the countertop and an empty bottle of baby aspirin with none to be seen amongst the sugar granules. Running upstairs to his room, she couldn't even think about what she might encounter, but there was George, quietly playing, totally unaware of the panic he was causing.

"Baby, where are all the pills from the baby aspirin bottle?" Donna managed to ask with bated breath.

"I ate them, Mommy. I couldn't sleep because my head hurt. I wanted some sugar in my tea, too," George calmly replied.

Donna couldn't even imagine how he had gotten the cap off the bottle. Relief at seeing him alive and, seemingly, none the worse for his little snack, mingled with fear of the unknown. She immediately called her pediatrician.

"Dr. Morgan, George got into the baby aspirin. I have no idea how many he took or what time he took them. He seems fine, now, but what can I do?" Donna tried to conceal her anxiety.

"Take him right to the Emergency Room," directed Dr. Morgan.

"It's too late to pump George's stomach," the Emergency Room doctor reported to a terrified Donna. "He looks OK now, but we'll have to admit him overnight for observation to make sure he doesn't have any drug toxicity. He hasn't had any ringing in his ears, which is an early sign of aspirin toxicity, so that's good, but we need to be sure he doesn't develop any other symptoms overnight."

"Okay," Donna agreed numbly.

George awoke the next day wondering why he was still in the hospital. "I'm fine, Mommy. I want to go home."

"You won't open any bottles again without Mommy or Daddy there, right?" Donna asked him, rather sternly.

"No," he answered, his head hanging sadly.

Through it all, she again kept saying to herself: "Not my child. Why did this have to happen to *my* child?"

In those days chowing down on St. Joseph's Aspirin for Children was not a particularly uncommon occurrence. Once a child was given one for a fever and he or she found out how good the little orange chewable pills tasted, they could seem like candy, enticing children to get that bottle open and eat them. But when it's your own child who does it, somehow things seem much worse. Another danger of an aspirin overdose is that, since that time, a connection has been found linking the use of aspirin in children to Reye's Syndrome. Reye's Syndrome is a rare condition that causes swelling in the brain and liver. It's good that wasn't known when George took them. That would have given his parents something else with which to concern themselves.

George weathered this near catastrophe, but he didn't stop worrying his parents.

"We need apples for the farm, Donna. I'm going to head to upstate New York after lunch," Tom told her.

"I think we'll go along. The boys have been begging for a ride in the tractor-trailer," she answered.

What Donna really wanted was some much-needed family time. The boys were excited because they would get to sleep in the sleeping cab of their tractor trailer, and four-year old George couldn't contain his excitement, jumping up and down in the cab.

"George, stop jumping and sit down!" said Donna. "You're going to get hurt! Come to me and let me put your pajamas on."

George obliged, but as soon as they were on, the jumping resumed, back and forth from the front to the back. Then it happened. During a jump, George's little hand landed on the door handle, and before Donna could intervene, the door opened, and George was gone.

Tom stopped the vehicle and Donna jumped down to see her son lying on the ground, awake and crying. The golf-ball sized goose egg on his head was unsettling, but he was alert and talking.

"Please hurry, Tom. We have to get up to New York so I can

call George's doctor," Donna pleaded.

Although seemingly unconcerned, as Donna would have expected from him, Tom did drive straight to their New York farm.

Dr. Morgan gave her instructions. "Make sure he is alert and talking. Put some ice on the lump, give him some acetaminophen for his headache and I'll see him in the morning."

For those of us in the emergency medicine field, this advice was quite reasonable. No loss of consciousness, alert and talking, he could wait until the morning to be seen. But for a young mom never having experienced this type of injury before, instead of sounding reassuring, to Donna he sounded unconcerned. "In the morning! Are you kidding?" she thought, angry and upset. The next morning, she was having trouble keeping George awake, and he seemed to be limp. At the same time, she was trying to watch 2 ½ year old Josh, but Tom wanted to stop to eat breakfast on the way back home.

"Donna, you're overreacting. He's limp, because he's tired. You've been waking him up all night. He'll be fine until we get back to New Jersey," Tom said impatiently when Donna objected to stopping on the way home.

Oblivious? Unconcerned? Donna didn't know, but she had spent the seemingly endless night trying to awaken George every 2 hours like the doctor had directed her to do. It was nighttime, and well past a four-year old's bedtime, so it is possible that he was just very sleepy. Unfortunately, when a head injury and sleep time coincide, there really is no way of knowing which one is causing the drowsiness without a medical provider's exam, and Donna didn't want to take any chances. It wasn't like he fell off a chair; he fell out of a moving truck onto a road and hit his head. That's scary. Donna felt like the trip home was playing out on a movie reel in slow motion, but they finally reached their home in New Jersey, and Donna immediately called their pediatrician. Without even waiting to hear what the doctor said, Tom headed off to work, seemingly unimpressed with little George's condition. Dr. Morgan, she felt, was equally unconcerned, and made her feel as if she was over-reacting, just as Tom had. Was she? By now she wasn't sure, either, but she didn't care. This was her baby and she wasn't going to let anyone make her feel stupid for worrying about him. Perhaps the doctor sensed Donna's panic and was trying not to add to her fears, but it came across as indifference to her. Tom did come home to take them to the hospital, as the pediatrician suggested, where George was admitted to the pediatrics unit of the hospital for observation. "Now that he is settled in his room, I'm going back to work," Tom said, nonchalantly.

"Fine," replied Donna, with an undisguised chill in her voice.

"My head hurts, Mommy," said George.

"Okay, baby. I'll have the nurses get you some medicine."

George took his medicine and fell asleep. Donna felt a little more relaxed and tried to rest herself, but rest didn't come easily. When your 4 ½ year old son is in the hospital after falling six feet from a moving vehicle and hitting his head on the road, it's hard to sleep. As the long day and night wore on, George became increasingly more restless and uncomfortable, sometimes screaming in pain, then falling silent.

"Nurse, something is wrong with George!" Donna said anxiously.

"Don't worry, Mrs. Gardner. I think he is just looking for attention. He seems to be fine," was her professional diagnosis and or lame attempt at comfort. By 2 AM, George was no better and nothing was being done about it. Frustrated, Donna picked up the phone and called Dr. Morgan herself. It wasn't exactly hospital protocol, but a mother has a certain awareness of her own children that others lack, professional healthcare providers or not, and she wasn't going to feel bad for cutting the red tape that night. It's amazing what an angry physician's orders can do to a nursing staff's response at 2:00 in the morning. The nurses went into fast forward mode, making George comfortable and rushing him to radiology for a brain scan, avoiding eye contact with Donna and Tom, who had arrived at that point.

Donna immediately noticed the grim look on Dr. Morgan's face as he walked into George's room after the brain scan.

"Tom and Donna, I'm sorry, but it appears that George has a large blood clot on his brain from his fall as well as an 8-inch skull fracture. I've called a neurosurgeon in because he will have to have the blood clot removed."

Donna felt like the world was crashing in around her as she listened to the doctor brief them on those two terrifying words: brain surgery. It seemed like a lifetime before the surgeon arrived. Donna tried to remain composed as George alternately laughed, screamed, blacked out, and fell asleep waiting for the neurosurgeon to arrive, and when he did, they immediately clicked. Donna and Tom liked him and felt a measure of comfort placing George in his hands. Donna signed the operative permit, understanding about every other word of what she was reading. What did it matter what it said? She had no choice. Her son was dying and there was no time for line item critical analysis. Besides, Tom read it, too, and he would have brought up any concerns. As she passed the signed permit to the surgeon, she grabbed his hand. "Please don't let my baby die," she pleaded with him. She held George's hand all the way up to the Operating Room until they allowed her to go no further.

"I'm scared, Mommy," cried George.

"I am too, Baby, but it's going to be alright," Donna said through her tears. "I love you."

"I love you, too, Mommy."

Donna's heart broke into a hundred pieces, and she closed her eyes and prayed, "Please, Lord. Don't let those be the last words I hear from my son. Please bring him through this surgery safely and whole. Please, don't let him die, not my child."

As she watched the stretcher disappear through the doorway, she could see his beautiful curly blonde locks disappear along with it. How many of those curls would be left after they shaved his little head? She didn't know if she would ever see him again or, if she did, if George would be the same little boy. She wondered how life could change so drastically, so quickly, so completely. She waited with feelings she found difficult to express. It felt surreal, almost as if she no longer owned her own body. Her brave little guy fought his way through the surgery with no obvious residual effects other than some temporary and intermittent visual disturbances. His little skull was still fragile from the fracture and he was required to wear a helmet for a while to protect it, but he made it through.

They had won another battle with George, but they were far from winning the war. Over the years he received diagnoses of ADD/ADHD, learning disabilities, bi-polar disorder, and to top it all off, primary immunodeficiency disorder (PID), which caused him to frequently be ill. PID, many times, results from a defect in the genetic code and is passed down from the parents. There are over 300 different kinds of immune disorders,[7] but the bottom line is that in PID the immune system cannot handle infection from bacteria and viruses as well as a healthy person's can. Autoimmune disorders are those in which the body thinks its own organs are the enemy and attacks them, causing inflammation and pain. One type of immune disorder is Lupus, from which Donna suffered and which gives credence to George's condition, since these diseases can be inherited. To account for his ongoing behavioral issues, the doctors felt he had sustained brain damage at some point in his life.

Donna, of course, blamed herself. She had had a lengthy labor, and although he seemed fine at birth, she wondered if he may have suffered from a lack of oxygen to the brain before he was born that was not immediately visible. Maybe it was that severe head injury that had caused bleeding in his brain when he was 4 ½ years old.

Whatever the root cause, George became increasingly sullen,

belligerent, angry, hateful, and rebellious throughout his teenage years. He started using drugs and alcohol. He didn't like the way the intravenous treatments for his PID made him feel, so he began to refuse them. He stopped his ADHD medication as well. He began to display hatred for Donna, his brother, Josh, who was two years younger, and even threatened to kill them, his dog, and his girlfriend. An involuntary commitment to a mental health facility was finally ordered, as George was a danger to himself and others. Donna did not even recognize her own son, anymore, and she was at a loss as to how to help him.

Tom didn't help matters because he thought that Donna was the problem. He supported George discontinuing his medications and was constantly paying his way out of trouble with bail bonds and lawyer fees.

The time came, however, when his father couldn't pay George's way out of trouble. A year after he graduated from high school, he and 35 other people were arrested for conspiracy to deliver drugs as part of a drug sting operation between New York and New Jersey. Taking into consideration George's mental health issues, the judge offered him a plea deal, but he refused to rat on his associates. Instead, the judge reduced the applicable sentence for this offense and sentenced him to six months in a federal camp, which is a minimum-security prison.

Guilt over George's troubles clawed at Donna like a fierce wild animal, only adding to her already low self-esteem. This stint in prison stopped George's drug trafficking but not his drug use, and that, combined with his bi-polar disorder, proved an ongoing challenge for him. He continued to have brushes with the law, and then finally, at around 40 years old, after counseling and maturity finally started working together, George settled down and became a productive member of society. And through all the trials and tribulations of George's life, that same burning thought kept recurring for Donna: "Not my child. Why did this happen to my child?"

These questions are part of grieving. My feeling is that victims are more likely to get stuck in the denial or anger stages of the grieving process because they are already using so much of their emotional energy to deal with their abusers and their own guilt. Maybe they just can't, or don't want to, accept that they must somehow conjure up more stamina for new challenges from their already depleted stores. Donna's silent questions were part denial and part anger, I believe, and it did take her years to work through it because the challenges in her life were relentless.

George and his trials were time-consuming, and Donna felt like she had not been paying enough attention to Josh, her younger son, and she was probably correct. Josh was two years younger than George and he did not have the problems or require the attention that his older brother did. He was a good boy and was spared the mental health issues that plagued his brother. He was also a source of support for Donna as he got older, which should not be the duty of one's offspring, but it does happen, probably more than we know. Josh was stuck in the middle of a blizzard, but seemed to be weathering it better than anyone, and therefore did not always receive the warmth he needed. This is what sometimes results when siblings or even students in school demonstrate a greater need for attention or services than other children. The squeaky wheels get the grease, and the children better equipped to handle themselves sometimes get left to their own devices, just because they are so capable of doing so. However, these children need attention, too, otherwise they can end up with problems, themselves. Josh did dabble in drugs but was not sucked into the larger drug and alcohol scene that George was. He is now, also, a productive member of society. What isn't obvious to the naked eye, though, is the resentment Donna reports that he has for her because of the unequal way her attention had to be distributed in the family. They are trying to make up for lost time, but it's a rocky road.

# Chapter 6

Sticks and Stones

Compounding the problems with her children, Donna, herself, continued to be inexplicably and frequently ill. As she had throughout childhood, she suffered from frequent infections, weight loss, anemia, fatigue, and musculoskeletal pain, but despite multiple doctors' exams and tests, no cause for her symptoms could be determined. These stressors impacted Donna and Tom's relationship to the point that the problems they were encountering began to outweigh whatever love had held them together. Tom had also started to drink and run around with other women, maybe to escape from the tension in the house and the responsibilities of having a high-maintenance child. The damage had been inflicted, and without healthy communication, which is essential to a marriage, their union ultimately ended in divorce, albeit amicably.

With the money Donna received from the divorce settlement, she purchased a little colonial style home. She took great delight in decorating and creating a cozy home for herself and her two sons,

George and Josh, and she loved it. People finally praised her for something: her flair for home décor. She was good at it and proud of herself for the first time in her life. However, she knew she couldn't support her little family with nothing but a flair for something, and she realized that she still needed gainful work. She didn't have a college education, and she had not learned or developed any marketable skills. She did, however, know how to clean, and began cleaning corporate offices, eventually establishing her own business, "Donna's Commercial Cleaning." She was alone but independent and successful. Her life seemed to be turning around, but the doctors still couldn't figure out what was physically wrong with her, which was increasingly frustrating. It was Saturday, and she had been having frequent attacks of severe abdominal pain, nausea, vomiting, and fever for the past several days and decided to go to the Emergency Room because her doctor's office was closed. She just couldn't imagine dealing with this pain all weekend.

Donna enjoyed drinking, but she was not an alcoholic. Unfortunately, her family history added to the assumptions doctors sometimes made about her and her unexplained symptoms.

"How much do you drink?" queried the Emergency Room doctor.

"I drink socially, and maybe a glass of wine a day," Donna truthfully responded.

"Now you need to be honest with us, Donna. Your gastrointestinal enzymes are through the roof, and we feel you have pancreatitis from excessive alcohol intake."

"I'm not an alcoholic," Donna insisted. "I know what an alcoholic is, and that's not me."

"Well, I don't know how else to explain these symptoms you are having and the elevated enzymes. They all point to pancreatitis from alcohol abuse."

"I've been sick all my life with symptoms that no one can explain, and I believe today is no different. I'm in pain, sick, and exhausted, and I resent being called an alcoholic when I'm not."

Donna was hoping to see a twinge of apology in the doctor's eyes, but she couldn't tell for sure. She had seen so many looks in medical providers' eyes over the years that she couldn't know for sure, anymore, what they were saying.

"Okay, well, regardless of the cause, we'll still have to admit you to the hospital for a few days. I'd like to see a few more tests ordered, and you need IV fluids and antibiotics. Once you get to feeling better and your test results improve, you can go home, but make sure you follow up with your doctor. We'll send the records of this visit to him."

Donna sighed and nodded her head. She expected this. She had been through it before.

Emergency rooms are designed to "treat 'em and street 'em." ER doctors are not there to take the place of family physicians, who have the luxury of knowing a patient's medical, social and family histories and the emotional components tied to all of them. They are there to diagnose and treat the urgent situation at hand, admit or discharge patients with proper instructions according to the current diagnosis, and advise them to follow up with their primary care physicians. Emergency room stretchers never get cold. When you are moved along, another patient will fill that bed within minutes. It's a process borne out of necessity as more and more people flood Emergency Rooms for care. You can't blame the medical providers, though. If you work in an ER long enough you often become programmed to make snap judgements. If a thin, fragile woman with jaundice, abdominal pain, and a family history of alcoholism turns up having elevated gastrointestinal enzymes, there is only one immediate conclusion: this patient is an alcoholic. Seasoned ER doctors have also learned that patients don't always tell the truth, like the pregnant teen who swears she "never had sex in her life." All this knowledge about the whys and the wherefores of Emergency Medicine is of little help to patients like Donna, however. Even trusted people can throw sticks and stones without realizing they are doing so, but the impact of the accusations and the resultant scars are still the same.

Donna did follow up with her doctors, as she had done in the past. Multiple medical doctors had thrown up their hands and then washed them clean of Donna's inexplicable illnesses, until someone, in frustration, sent her to see a psychiatrist, knocking an already fragile self-esteem even further down into the hole.

The psychiatrist she was seeing, Dr. Brian, threw her a lifeline. "Donna, you aren't crazy," Dr. Brian said. "I think I have an idea of what could be going on with you."

Donna was skeptical. "Really? How can a psychiatrist figure

out what tons of other doctors couldn't?"

"Well, it's just a hunch, but I think you may have Lupus," he said.

"Why would that not have shown up on any of the tests I had done?" Donna asked with an earned degree of suspicion.

"Lupus Erythematosus, or LE, is an autoimmune disorder that can be difficult to diagnose, as many of them are," he answered. "You must be in an exacerbation, or flare-up, of the disease before the markers for inflammation will show up, and since no one suspected it when you were sick, they didn't test for it. Even if someone had done a routine test for it, the results would be normal if you weren't sick at the time. LE is also a diagnosis of exclusion, meaning that it should be considered from the history of symptoms and family history when all other illnesses have been ruled out."

Finally, a possible explanation for Donna's misery. A diagnosis of Lupus isn't optimum, but it was something tangible to explain what was going on with her. The moment she heard a real diagnosis, she felt like the wrecking ball that had been destroying her life had finally been shattered. The symptoms fit, right down to her elevated enzymes in the hospital.

"Have I had this since I was a child?" she asked. "Is this why I was so sick all the time, even then?"

"It's possible," said Dr. Brian. "There is no cure for Lupus, but we can develop a treatment plan that might help you manage your symptoms." Donna was relieved and happy to know she wasn't crazy. She felt like she had just been released from the prison in which her body had been held hostage. She began treatments and, although she knew her illness was incurable, she was feeling better and showing amazing resilience, despite the pain and insecurity she had endured as a child that had knocked her down. Donna was happier and seemed to be traveling a road less bumpy for now.

Contrary to what some doctors believed before new evidence came to light, autoimmune disorders are not caused by a damaged emotional state. In the past, depression was a common diagnosis for the group of symptoms with which people presented that could not be explained by qualifiable test results. Because people became understandably depressed having to deal with illnesses that no one could identify and thinking that no one believed them, they were labelled as depressants. On the other side of that coin, however, the mental state of a person can, indeed, worsen the symptoms of Lupus and other autoimmune disorders. A person may have more than one of these autoimmune illnesses plaguing their body at the same time, and they do tend to run in families. People who suffer from one or more entities within this set of immune system disorders need to keep their lives as stress-free as possible. In the state of Donna's life, all her life, she had plenty of triggers for her Lupus flares.

# Chapter 7

A Shattered Dream

After Donna divorced Tom and before she met Max, she was generally satisfied with her life at first, but she had never stopped thinking about her firstborn, that little boy with whom she was able to share only a few stolen moments before he was given to new parents. When he turned18 years old, the legal age for adulthood in New Jersey, she intended to find him. She had remained in contact with a social worker, from whom she learned he had been adopted into an Italian home and bore the same hair, eyes, and coloring as his adoptive parents. However, just because a couple is vetted by social services and approved to adopt a child in the present doesn't automatically mean they have been granted a future good parent seal of approval. Donna's son's adoptive parents, Antonio and Grace, do not appear to have been in the running for that one. His mother wasn't always nice, and his father ran around on her. The social worker had told Donna that her son was a troubled child and that he knew he was adopted and had wanted to find his biological mother, but Grace refused to allow it. She learned that Antonio and Grace had another son after Ronnie, but his father left his mother and her two sons for another woman and they divorced when Ronnie was just six years old.

I find it interesting that Donna's biological son ended up in a family not unlike her own: a difficult mother and a father who ran around on her. Different lives with similar outcomes. In this instance, we can see both nature and nurture at work. We don't know what Ronnie's biological father would have been like had he stayed in their lives, but Ronnie's biological grandfather, Mario, had a similar approach to marriage. It invites the question of how Ronnie's genetic makeup would have been expressed in a family that was more nurturing with different role models.

Donna couldn't legally contact her son while he was still a minor, but on his 18th birthday, she called the social services agency to talk to her social worker and was devastated to learn of her passing. The bittersweet silver lining to that cloud was that Donna was informed that one of her social worker's dying wishes was that she be reunited with her son, Ronnie, on his 18th birthday. She was able to locate him, and they spoke a few times on the phone, then planned to meet. Grace picked up the phone the day Donna called to make the plans.

"Hello?"

"Hello, my name is Donna Miflin. I'm Ronnie's biological mother. I believe he has told you that we've spoken on the phone already, and we would like to meet. May I speak with him, please?"

The revelation apparently stunned Grace, and it took her a few minutes to compose herself enough to decide what she wanted to say.

"How dare you? How dare you call this house? How did you know how to find us?! You should not have been given that information! I'll sue you for contacting us! I will NOT allow you to see Ronnie! You haven't been his mother for 18 years, I have!"

"I don't want to disrupt your life. I only want to meet him. He deserves to know who I am if he wants to."

"He doesn't know what he wants, and he doesn't know what's good for him, either! He doesn't need you in his life!"

"Mom, what's going on out here? Who are you yelling at?" Donna heard a young man's voice say. Her heart quickened.

"Nobody. Don't worry about it. It doesn't concern you," Grace said, quickly.

"Well, I think it does concern me. That's my biological mother on the phone, isn't it?" Ronnie said.

Grace couldn't deny what Ronnie had already heard.

"Yes. She said you had already talked, and you didn't tell me!? Why didn't you tell me? She wants to meet you," Grace said flatly.

Donna didn't know that Grace was unaware of their correspondence, so she waited until the conversation between Ronnie and his mother was over before rejoining the discussion.

"When can we do that? I want to meet her, too. I'm 18 and if you won't let me talk to her, I'll find her myself somehow."

"Please," Donna said. "He wants to meet me. What can it hurt?"

After an awkward silence, Grace said to Ronnie, "OK, but only if I meet her first."

"Really? I'm not a child, anymore, Mom."

"That's the way it will be," Grace said, sternly.

Donna met Grace at a deli on the corner of a busy downtown street in Trenton, New Jersey. Describing their meeting as awkward wouldn't do it justice. They had described themselves to each other, so they knew who to look for. Donna had gotten there a little early and was sipping her coffee when Grace arrived.

"Are you Donna?" Grace asked, stiffly.

"Yes, are you Ronnie's mother?"

"It's Grace. Yes."

"Grace, thank you for meeting me. Do you have any questions for me?" asked Donna.

"Well, I want to know why you want to see Ronnie. You gave him up and adoptions are supposed to be private. I'm the only mother he has ever known. What do you want from him?"

"I don't want anything from him; I just want to meet him, see who he has become. I was 16 when I had him. I wish I could have kept him then, but I couldn't. Giving him up was the best thing for him. I couldn't care for him, and I want to thank you for doing that." Donna was sincere about what she was feeling but based on the few minutes she had spoken with Grace she wasn't surprised that Ronnie was troubled.

Grace brought out some pictures of Ronnie to show Donna. It

occurred to her that this was going to be all Grace would offer her in the way of meeting her son.

"Here." Grace pushed the photos over to Donna. "Seeing you, I don't know why Ronnie is so heavy. Was his father heavy?"

"No," Donna answered, "but I haven't seen him since then. He went to Vietnam and I haven't talked to him since he got back."

"Oh." Grace did tell Donna some highlights of Ronnie's life and Donna told her about her boys, but it was all very strained.

"Well, now you know what you want to know about him, and you saw pictures of him. That should be enough for you." Grace got up to leave.

"No," said Donna. "I want to meet him."

"Well, that won't happen on my watch," Grace replied. "You're on your own. If you want to see him, you can figure it out without my help."

Shocked and saddened, Donna watched Grace disappear through the doors along with her hope of seeing Ronnie.

Eventually, Donna and Ronnie found their way to each other. Ronnie was about to leave for Marine training when they finally met, and they kept in touch while he was gone. She was grateful to finally see that baby boy she kissed goodbye all those years ago, and she will never forget the nurse, Jean, that made that happen for her. She was eager to tell George and Josh about their half-brother. One day she received a phone call from him telling her about the girl he had met and was going to marry. She was overjoyed. She had found her son and would now have a daughter-in-law. She was even happier when she got the call that she was going to be a grandmother. When the baby was born, Donna boarded the next plane to Kentucky to help them out. She had a daughter-in-law and a baby granddaughter to meet.

Donna was happy when Ronnie and his wife, Sarah, moved back to New Jersey. They moved in with Grace, but things did not go smoothly for them. They continually argued and Ronnie was not treating his wife well. When Sarah became pregnant a second time, Ronnie wanted nothing to do with the new baby, or his wife and daughter, and left. I verified with Donna that the baby was Ronnie's; he just didn't want it. Like his adoptive daddy before him, and his biological grandfather, Mario, Ronnie had a girlfriend and went to live with her. His pregnant wife and daughter packed up and moved in with a friend until the baby's birth, an event Ronnie did not deem important enough to attend.

A couple of years later, Grace became ill with lung cancer and subsequently died. Donna had married her second husband, Max, by then, and the two of them went to pick up Sarah and the children for the funeral, but soon learned that Ronnie didn't want his little family there. Donna was disappointed in Ronnie, but Sarah still wanted to attend, so Donna and Max took their grandchildren home with them, only to receive an anguished phone call from Sarah after the funeral. Ronnie had brought "the other woman" to the gathering at his mom's house and he and Sarah were not even divorced yet. He had ignored Sarah the entire day except to tell her not to bring the children. He didn't even want them at the house after the funeral to be with the rest of Grace's family.

"Ronnie," Donna said when he picked up the phone at his mother's house. "When are you coming for the kids. They're getting tired and cranky and they should be there with the family. They are your children."

"I don't want them here," Ronnie answered, "so I won't be picking them up."

"Ronnie, this is just wrong. I'm sorry about your mother, but your children have a right to be there with the rest of the family. Your actions are totally inappropriate. Your children are important."

"Oh, fuck off, Donna. You don't have the right to tell me what to do with my own family," said Ronnie.

"Oh, so what was I to you then, just a meal ticket?" asked Donna, who had been helping them out financially when money was tight. Her irritation with Ronnie was growing.

"Pretty much."

And that was it. Donna and her son, Josh, took the children and dropped them off with Sarah. Donna has not spoken with Ronnie since that night.

Ronnie went on to divorce Sarah, get remarried, and start a whole new life, remaining as far away from his previous life as he could. Ronnie was close to his father, though, the one who had left them when he was six, so it begs the question of why he behaved like he did: taking no responsibility for his children, disrespecting his wife, and seeking greener grass in other yards.

It's a well-known fact that children mimic what they see at home. Even babies start to do this by imitating movements like sticking out a tongue. Throughout childhood, mental notes are being kept, consciously or unconsciously, on the behavior, attitudes, and problem-solving techniques of our parents. It could suggest one reason why Ronnie, in an unhappy marriage, chose to take the same road his adoptive father, Antonio, had: leaving his family. Research has repeatedly shown that children of divorce are more likely to be divorced themselves, however, that doesn't have to be a self-fulfilling prophesy.[8] Some adult children see undesirable character traits in their parents and choose to do the opposite as parents themselves, and others model their parent's behavior. Ronnie didn't want to be with his wife and children in the first place, so he may have felt a bond with his father by repeating his behavior. It's also possible that a loving relationship may be able to withstand the effects of a parent's negative influence.

We all know that there are two sides to every coin; it's never just one person's fault when a relationship fails. The nature versus nurture character development scale is lopsided, and so is the blame scale, because no one is perfect. Considering this, even if Sarah would have been a terrible person, Ronnie's children were still his responsibility, no matter what. Parents should not punish their children for mistakes they made with each other. Children don't ask to be brought into this world; we decide to bring them here. They are faultless at birth and deserve, no, are owed, every bit of love and support they can get from the adults who created them or who have accepted the responsibility of becoming their parents. Life is tough enough to begin with. Cycles of abuse and poor role modeling must end somewhere along the line for positive outcomes in life to begin. If this is you, you still have a chance to change and break that cycle. Find a good counselor who can help you explore what it is that is preventing you from breaking free. If you are a parent, think of things your parents might have done wrong and don't repeat them with your children. Listen to your children, spend time with them, laugh with them and cry with them, but most of all love them.

# Chapter 8

They Meet

The phone was ringing. Tripping over a stool to get to the phone so as not to miss any business, Donna grabbed the receiver.

"Hello, Donna's Commercial Cleaning, Donna Gardner speaking."

"Hello, Donna. My name is Max Miflin. I believe we met at my father's office building when you were cleaning there, and I have a few offices in the same building. You seem to do a good job. Do you have any openings to clean mine?"

"I think I do," Donna replied. "Let me look at my schedule." Donna flipped through a few pages. "Yes, I do. I'll get you set up."

Donna was excited. She was happy for the business, and she had also seen Max in the office when she came in to clean. He was in great shape, had muscles, and was rather good looking. She had heard that he was an athlete, and she believed it by looking at him.

She set Max up with a schedule to clean his office, and a new dance began for her.

It's hard to appear sexy and glamorous in a cleaning uniform, but she made sure that her uniform was clean and pressed the days she went to clean Max's office. She always made sure that she presented well, anyway, but she took extra care on those days. She made sure she jazzed up anything she could, her hair, her nails, and her make-up. Max wasn't there the first couple of times but one day he was there working late when she showed up. She greeted him with a smile and a cordial "Hello" which he returned. While she was cleaning, she caught him stealing glances in her direction. She didn't want to seem too obvious, but she couldn't help but notice those eyes, dark and intense. After that, it seemed he was working late every time she was there, and every time, they would share glances and engage in some small talk.

After a while he asked her if she would be willing to come and clean his private home.

"Sure," she said, and they set up a schedule for that, too. When she walked into his home the first time, she was taken aback by its size and elegance. It was surely an executive's home, like the kind that only existed in dreams in her world. It didn't take long, after that, for Max to ask Donna on a date. She was beside herself with excitement. How could she have landed a date with this tall, handsome, successful man? He picked her up that night and when she opened the door, he just stared at her. She had purchased a new outfit, famously known as "the little black dress." It was sleek and off-the-shoulder, with a black silk rose attached to a top that dipped down her chest just low enough to be tantalizing but not enough to seem slutty. The back was open, but the dress covered just as much as it had to, to be classy. She had chosen her accessories expertly, and he examined her from the top of her beautifully styled hair down to her black stiletto heels. While he was admiring her, she was admiring him, as well. She soaked in the picture of the charcoal-colored turtleneck sweater that conformed to his tight body. His trousers were immaculate and had not one wrinkle. His shoes were polished to look like new. Donna had to pinch herself to make sure she wasn't dreaming.

Donna let him in the house, and he handed her a bouquet of red roses that looked stunning with her black outfit, a fact Max did not fail to notice.

"You look gorgeous," he said. "Can you wear that the next time you come to clean?"

Donna laughed at the thought.

"If you pay me double, maybe," she joked back.

The night was magical. They went to a chic restaurant and sat down at a little table away from everyone else. A candle burned in the center and soft music played in the background. It could not have been more romantic. Max was funny and had Donna laughing all evening. He told her about his love for baseball and how he was helping his father build the business. As they talked, the waiter kept coming back to see if they needed anything else. They knew the restaurant was about to close, so Max left a generous tip, complimented the waiter on a job well-done, and rose to leave. The busboys were at their table before they even got to the door. Donna couldn't fail to notice how well he treated everyone.

Max pulled his Mercedes up to the curb in front of her house and got out. He rushed around to her side so he could open her door and walked her up to the porch.

"Thank you, Max. I had a wonderful time," said Donna.

"You're very welcome. I did, too."

He looked at her for a minute, then cupped her face in his hands and delivered a soft sensual kiss to her lips. She felt like she was melting right there in his arms.

"Same time next week?" asked Max.

"Yes, I would like that very much."

The next few dates were great. They had fun and got to know each other. There was only Max and his son, Carl, living in their house, so it didn't get very dirty, but Donna still came every week. She had a key to his home in case he was out when she arrived.

"Max, I'm here," called Donna. She always announced herself when she came in to clean.

"I'll be right down," Max called back. "You know, the house isn't very dirty. Carl has been at his grandparents' home all week, and I haven't been around much. How about if we just have a glass of wine and relax?"

"Okay, that sounds good," said Donna.

Max put some soft rock on the radio, poured two glasses of dry white wine, and they sat down and talked for a while. The wine bottle was almost empty when Max drew Donna close to him and repeated the soft kiss that he gave her on their first date, but today it was longer, more passionate than before. She responded in kind and they embraced each other like they never wanted to let go. He held her head in his hands, then found her neck with his lips, opening the buttons on her shirt at the same time. His hands and lips gently moved down to her breasts, caressing them and showering them with soft kisses. Her conscience was no match for this electricity, and they both gave in to their desires, burning as hot as the fireplace that had been setting the stage.

Their story was starting out like a fairy tale with passionate sex, romantic dinners, fun, flowers and gifts. But lying in wait, below this tapestry of charm, was a darker side of Max that Donna had begun to uncover but was choosing to deny. As he became more comfortable and confident with her, she began to see how much alcohol he consumed and how he couldn't go without a drink for too long. Cognac was his evening drink of choice, but Donna began to suspect it didn't stop there. Worse yet, his behavior was becoming erratic, and he started asking her to go with him to parties where she knew people would be doing drugs. She was aware of Max's drinking and that he had been introduced to marijuana and cocaine while he was still in college, but she never thought it would get out of hand, as it seemed to be doing. He was becoming impatient, critical, and cruel to her, and she was devastated. Donna's low self-esteem made her think that, somehow, she had caused this change in Max. She even started to do some cocaine with him because she thought that he would be happier with her if she shared in his vices. As the beautiful tapestry she and Max had begun to weave together began to unravel, she saw him for the man he really was, an erratic, egotistical, and narcissistic drug addict, alcoholic, and womanizer. She knew he liked to flirt with women—a lot—but she considered it harmless. It was just "Max being Max." She remembered the Max she'd just met, and she thought that surely, she could fix him.

But it didn't get better. The words he would throw at her over their collective time together, before and after they were married, stung. Cunt. Fucking cunt. Bitch. Ugly Bitch, Auschwitz Bitch, Trailer Park Trash. Worthless. Dumb. Stupid. Simple.

*"You are an awful mother."*

*"No one else would want you."*

*"You will wind up like your mother and sister."*

*"You are going down."*

*"I wish you were dead."*

*"You have no friends. No one likes you."*

*"If it wasn't for me, you'd have nothing."*

*"You are going to jail."*

*"If I go, you are going with me. I'll make your death look like an accident."*

*"I'm really not this person. You're the one who makes me act like this."*

This was Donna's love now, and these are the terms of endearment that Max had been, and would be in the future, bestowing upon her. This verbal abuse started even before they got married, but Donna believed his lies that their problems were all her fault. Even after Max proposed to her and she accepted, a persistent, nagging doubt was, for the most part, ignored. Abusers are master manipulators. They are bullies, generally choosing victims who are weaker physically and/or emotionally than they. The more someone hears how bad they are, the more they believe it, and the more tethered to the stronger person they become, because they have been programmed to believe they can't make it on their own. I'll bet many of you can still repeat your multiplication tables without even thinking about it. This resulted from repetition—being told repeatedly how much 5x3 is. The same principle can work with lies, too, such as believing you are worthless, if this is what you are continually being told. For victims, isolation makes this even worse, because there is no positive reinforcement to counteract the negative. The abuser does not want any friends or extended family telling their victims just how strong they really are or can be.

Verbal abuse can come as outright degradations or disguised as jokes to make people laugh at the victim's expense. Have any of you ever watched a roast on TV? I dislike them intensely because it is humor that exploits someone's shortcomings for the entertainment of others. Now, I understand that the "victims" accept these barrages of personal assaults willingly, sometimes because the roast is serving to benefit a charity, and that's on them, but many a truth is said in jest, and the truth sometimes silently hurts. Can you imagine enduring this type of levity at your expense on a regular basis, true or not? To see this at work, we only must look as far as Max and Donna's relationship, except there were no valid jokes, only the ones in Max's mind.

The tipping point for Donna came at what seemed like a typical party.

"Hey, Cunt, get me another drink, and make sure you don't spill it this time," Max barked at Donna as he and his friends partied on the beach one evening. She hadn't really wanted to go to this private party to begin with, but she went, anyway, a decision she later regretted.

"That stupid wench can't even hold her liquor when it's in a glass," Max cackled to his friends, resulting in the desired response of drunken laughter around the bonfire they had made.

"Coming up, Max," said Donna quickly, and she rushed off to fulfill his command.

Between the drugs and booze, she was surprised no one wound up in the Emergency Room with burns from the fire.

When she returned with his drink, Max was sitting in between two young women, laughing, and posturing to show off his masculine physique.

"Max, what's going on?" Donna yelled as she delivered his drink.

"Oh, shut up, you dumb Bitch. It's nothing," Max answered as he drew in a line of cocaine. "They may be prettier than you, but you're a better fuck."

His drunk and high cronies howled with laughter.

"Max, I can't take this anymore. You are so wasted you don't even care what you're doing." Donna replied, so angry she could hardly think straight. "You have to get help."

"For what? For something that makes me happy? Partying makes me happy. Are you going to make me happy?" he snickered sarcastically, blowing a kiss in her direction. "Go ahead. Leave. Who else will want you? You have no friends. What would you do without me?"

Donna stormed off the beach and went home by herself. It was becoming apparent to her that the emotional abuse was showing no signs of letting up, like a persistent thunderstorm on the day of a huge outdoor party. The abyss into which Max was falling was deeper than Donna had imagined, and she hadn't the strength to pull him out of it. She had had enough. She left and went home, vowing that this was it. She was going to leave him. She began to summon up the courage to finally make a clean break, but upcoming circumstances would not favor this plan.

She awoke with a relentless hangover the morning after the beach party. "Oh, I can't party like that again," Donna thought.

She thought that vomiting a few times would help, but it didn't, the awful nausea continued. Crackers and ginger ale helped a little, but not for long. She felt a bit better as the day wore on, ate some soup and laid down for a nap. By the evening she was feeling significantly better and she believed she was out of the woods, but the next morning the nausea and vomiting recurred with a vengeance. She picked up the phone and called her doctor, who was able to get her on the schedule within an hour.

"We'll run some blood work, Donna. It's probably just a stomach bug, but because of your Lupus, I just want to make sure I don't miss anything," Dr. Patel told her after her exam. "I'll call you when the results come back. Just keep your diet light for now. Eat bland foods, no spicy, greasy, fried, or fatty foods, and drink small, frequent amounts of fluids to stay hydrated until we find out what the problem is."

Donna nodded and thanked him, unfazed. She was accustomed to doctors not knowing what was wrong with her. At least it wasn't appendicitis or something else more serious that would have required her to go to the emergency room again. If she never saw another emergency room in her life she would be satisfied.

Donna felt no better when she woke up in the morning. She was tiring of being sick. Her stomach was churning when Dr. Patel called.

"Your blood work all looks normal Donna, for which we can be grateful, but when was your last menstrual period?"

It was late, she told him, but she was never regular.

"Well, I can tell you that your nausea and vomiting will most likely subside in a month or so. You're pregnant. I want you to make an appointment with your OB-GYN doctor's office for your first prenatal visit as soon as you can. They will probably consider you a high-risk pregnancy, so it will be important to bring your doctor on board as soon as you can. Congratulations."

Donna thanked him and hung up the phone, stunned and scared, her stomach churning even more. She had just about mustered up enough courage to get away from Max and now this. She confided to Gina all the unpleasant details of her relationship with Max and her intense fear of the future.

"Get away from him," Gina said. "I hear the way he speaks to you. Is he abusing you?"

"He's not hitting me, Mom. It's just in his words."

"I don't care. That's as bad as being hit and you never know when or if that will happen. That drug use of his is going to be the end of both of you. Leave him."

"I can't, anymore," Donna meekly admitted. "I'm pregnant, Mom. I don't have the means or the strength to handle another baby and the boys by myself."

"Oh, no. Donna, how did you get pregnant again? You're not 15 years old, anymore. Weren't you taking precautions?"

"I was. I had a diaphragm in, but then I lost weight while I was sick and it didn't fit right, anymore, so it didn't work the way it was supposed to."

"It doesn't matter, anyway. You still can't stay with him," Gina replied, unsympathetically.

"I have to. I don't have a choice," Donna said.

George and Josh were not little boys anymore, but they still required significant time and attention. Then there was Max's son from his first marriage. How could she leave Carl alone with Max, knowing who he was?

Donna's mind and her body were constantly disagreeing with

each other, making it difficult for her to make healthy choices. She was weak and sick and getting treatments for her illness but she could not stop herself from longing for the security that marriage and a home represented, or for Max, himself. In her weakened physical state, it was all she could do to take care of herself and her children, let alone plan an exit strategy. Even though he abused her, Max was still a living, breathing warm body in the house to be of whatever help he was worth. She couldn't work, pay medical bills on her own and still take care of her children, so what could she have done? And he didn't even have to be nice to keep her there—she was stuck.

The pain and insecurities of her life eventually drove Donna to therapy, but most of it focused on her attempts to determine what it was that *she* was doing wrong, of course. She had spent all her life feeling worthless; why should it be any different now? She still believed Max's lies and disregarded her counselor's advice to leave him, continuing to try to fix *herself,* because after his repeated slurs on her character, she truly believed it was all her fault, believed his lies. In between the demeaning verbal attacks, however, there was charm, flowing like a clear stream, complete with tears, gifts, apologies and promises of change, and she bought his smooth-talk every time, as do so many other women with their abusers. "I don't know what happened to me that day. I promise I will never hit you again. That's not me." These are just a few of the apologetic words that could have been taken from the script of any abuser's play. The funny thing is that some men truly mean it when they say it, but they have triggers that just light up their anger like a piece of paper thrown into the fireplace, and they can't conquer them.

Donna described Max as a great maker-upper. Sweet talk, affection, flowers and jewelry were all part of Max's charm, but if you looked beyond the outward clarity of his stream of charm, the waters were murky, sharp rocks and stones would become visible, and you couldn't tell in which direction the waters would carry him next. Through all of it, a part of Donna still thought she could help to pull him out of the deep substance abuse chasm into which he had fallen, and she was determined to do her best to try. He was only like that when he was drunk or high, right? Despite it all, they loved each other, right? She could do this; she was sure she could. She had been looking for love, security, and a happy family, all the things she was denied as a child, and she wanted it desperately, deserved it, even, and she was going to do her level best to make it happen, but it wasn't her destiny to ride off in a gilded pumpkin carriage with one dainty glass slipper. Instead, the clock struck 12 before she knew it, and she became locked inside the walls of the slowly rotting pumpkin.

# Chapter 9

Escalation

Donna had misgivings about marrying Max, but, being pregnant and sick, she didn't feel there was a way out, so against her own instincts and in the face of Gina's objections, she married Max, and they created a family of his, hers, and theirs. Max could be charming, as Donna already knew, and he didn't hesitate to use it to accomplish his personal goals.

"Gina, I have something to ask you. I know you don't approve of Donna marrying me, but I promise you I will take good care of her and the boys. I love her, and I'll prove to you and her that I can be a worthy husband and step-father."

Gina looked at Max suspiciously. She had heard her share of empty promises.

"I want to give them a nice home," he continued, "but I need a loan and the bank won't give it to me because of problems with the business. Would you be able to loan me the money to put a down-payment on a house? You can live with us and I will make a payment to you every month until it is paid back. I want to make a good family home for all of us."

"Max, I don't believe a word you are saying," said Gina, "but this time, I am going to give you the benefit of the doubt. I wasn't there for Donna when she was growing up and this is my chance to try and make it up to her. She needs someone to take care of her and help her, and I don't believe that you are that person. I love her and the boys and you have to promise me you will be good to them and never lay a hand on any of them."

"I promise, Gina. I'm going to change, but please don't tell Donna about this." She surmised that would make him seem weak in Donna's eyes, something he definitely did not want to do.

Donna sold her beloved little Dutch Colonial home, and between that money and Gina's secret money they built a beautiful, big custom home in a wealthy Mahwah, New Jersey community. One thing Max did right, although he may not have had a choice in the matter, was to put the home in Donna's name, protecting the investment from creditors who would try to seize it to pay off the business debt. Max inviting Gina to live with them was a big help to Donna, especially with baby Alex, but, at the same time, it removed some of the responsibility that she and the boys presented off his broad, yet essentially weak, shoulders.

Donna called Gina her buffer. She could stand up to Max when Donna couldn't. Sometimes she would round up Donna and Alex, like a mother hen protecting her chicks, and take them into her bedroom to get away when Max was on one of his drunken or high tirades downstairs. Sometimes he would be in a rant, and partway through his raging, Gina would appear, and Max would stop dead in his tracks like he had hit a stone wall when he saw her face. When served with divorce papers or a restraining order, he would turn on the charm filter for Gina, hoping he could bring her over to his side of the pool, but as soon as she asked him to start repaying the loan, the filter was immediately turned off and the water became dirty once again. When Donna had her bouts with Lupus, Gina took care of her. When Max cut Donna off from the checkbook or charge cards, Gina went grocery shopping and paid the bills. When Max was out partying, she took care of all of them. Gina was Donna's savior. Donna is certain that she would be dead right now had it not been for her mother. Gina was a deterrent to Max's behavior, but she was no match for his strength, especially while he was impaired. There were times she was gone from the house, or just couldn't stop him, and all she could do was give him dirty looks and hope for the best. She was afraid of him, too, when he was in this state. Donna was finally feeling close to her mom, but she also felt guilty for putting her in this position to begin with.

Once again, Donna just didn't feel like she fit into the elite lifestyle of their new community. As happy as she was with her new little son, Max had not changed, accentuating his empty promises. Max did enter a drug rehab program after Alex was born, but the birth of his new baby hindered, instead of contributed to, Max's recovery. In fact, the added responsibilities of another child and omnipresent mother-in-law seemed to make things worse and gave him even more incentive to escape from reality. This reconfiguring of a life would be an adjustment for anyone with even the most stellar mental health, but for people like Donna and Max, it was a significant challenge.

He continued to spiral out of control, as did his relationships with Donna's two boys, George and Josh, who were now 18 and 20 years old. Max's escalating drunken tirades were of increasing concern for them. They were protective of their mom and were worried about her safety. When Donna first married Max, they all got along for the most part, but it wasn't long before George and Josh couldn't escape seeing, or being subjected to, his erratic behavior and fury any more than Donna could. He was nice to them one minute, and then, without the slightest provocation, lashed out at them, mirroring his treatment of their mother.

"What the fuck are you doing, eating a sandwich in the middle of the day? It's not supper!" Max screamed at George. "You guys are nothing but consumers, eating the food I pay for, using whatever you need around the house! Go out and get a job!"

George knew his mom would pay a heavy price if he struck Max, so he refrained from acting on his feelings.

"I didn't have breakfast," he lied.

"Well, watch how much you eat around here. Food is expensive," Max grumbled.

This is how it was in the Miflin household. Max was becoming angrier and more frightening as time went on. Admittedly, the boys were no angels either, but everything they did was eliciting worsening angry reactions from Max. He was also jealous of Donna's relationship with all the boys. He suspiciously watched Donna, George, and Josh talking in the living room one day as paranoia had begun to infect Max's perception of reality and fuel his anger. "Hey. What are you three in a huddle about? Are you talking about me again? I know what you think of me, that it's always my fault. But it isn't. I'm this way because of her. She drives me to this! You two always side with your mom and never with me, no matter what! And Donna, you worry so much about their problems, but what about mine? I need help, too, but all you care about is them. You don't care about me at all. You're all just a bunch of fucking Benedict Arnolds! Are you asking them to cover up for you, Slut? Why? Did your boyfriend just call?" Max screamed in a drunken fit.

"Max, I'm not cheating on you. How could I? You know what I'm doing every minute of the day. You think I don't know about the cameras you had installed in the house? You take away my car keys, take away the checkbook, freeze my charge cards, have the phone turned off. How can I be doing anything while I'm stuck here? You're stalking me!" argued Donna.

"How could I be stalking you? I'm your husband! I have a right to know where you are and what you do, especially if it affects me! I don't believe you're not stepping out on me. I'll get something on you, Cunt! I know you are seeing someone. I don't know who but I'm going to find out and you'll both be sorry!"

Max grabbed his car keys, and Donna's as well, and slammed the door so hard on the way out that the fine crystal in the hutch tinkled as the glasses knocked against each other. The car screeched out of the driveway, and he was on his way out in search of love and acceptance from his drunk or high friends and easy women. Donna just let him go. There was no sense in defending herself, because when Max was in this state, it was impossible to reason with him. George and Josh knew better than to interfere, but they stayed until he left to make sure their mom was OK.

It wasn't unusual for Max to take Donna's keys away from her. That way he had complete control over her whereabouts and could ensure she was isolated from anyone who might hear about her plight and try to help her. Isolating someone from outside contacts is a common tactic for abusers to control their victims and being isolated is a lonely state in which to live. It may sometimes be the first sign of a problem and can be insidious in its onset. Isolating a person effectively removes any source of competition for the victim's attention. Victims are often cut off from their family and friends, sometimes even made to quit jobs so that the spotlight remains on the abuser, and no one else, in a victim's eyes. An abuser can make a victim believe that she doesn't need friends, that all she needs is him. Isolation can deprive a woman of the source of financial support that she might need to get away from her abuser. Consider that an abusive relationship is all about control, dominance, aggression, and fearmongering by any means necessary, and isolating someone seems like the perfect approach to accomplish those goals. Certainly, physical violence is the one most identifiable player in cases of domestic violence, but abuse isn't always physical. It can be emotional or sexual, too, and isolation is emotional abuse.

As often happens in abuse situations, Max felt remorse for his angry outburst the next day. He prepared a candlelight dinner for Donna, complete with flowers and music, attempting to atone for his actions, and, admittedly, setting the stage for some cozy "dessert" afterwards. In Max's journals, he claims to have had a sex addiction. He wrote that sex drove every decision he made, as it was with his decision to treat Donna to dinner that night. Maybe it was too little, too late, or maybe she saw through the guise and was not in the mood for "dessert," but he claims she was on the phone for two hours and finally, the night not fulfilling his desires and expectations, he stormed out with a "Fuck it! Fuck you!" Naturally, he felt this gave him a get out of jail free card to do what he wanted that night. He states he felt "left out, shunned, and ignored," which drove him out to party. Booze, drugs, girls, and friends that understood him was the whole ball of wax for Max, and all because his family didn't treat him the way he wanted, never considering how his own actions contributed to the rejection, typical of a narcissistic personality.

Later that night, Max walked through the door, emboldened by whatever satisfying escapades he had experienced. "Why do you make me do these things?" he yelled at Donna. "I'm not this person, but you drive me crazy! If it wasn't for you, I would probably be sober!"

"Don't you put that on me!" Donna returned. "You started doing this stuff long before you even met me. I'm sorry that I do things to get you mad, but I'm not the cause of your problems."

"All I wanted was a little appreciation for all the trouble I went through to make this dinner for you and some sex afterwards, but you couldn't even do that!"

Max was getting louder and angrier by the minute.

"I don't know why I stay with you," Donna said. "Everyone tells me I should leave you and I don't know why I don't."

"Everyone who!" Max questioned her, grabbing her arms. "Your Mom? Your freeloader sons? Your friends, if you even have any?"

"Everyone," Donna replied, trembling, her bravery waning.

Max's adrenaline-infused paranoia took the reins and he tossed Donna's fragile body up against the wall. She doubled over in pain and could barely walk. Stunned at what he had done, Max drove her to the hospital.

"What happened?" the triage nurse in the Emergency Room asked.

"I slipped on the floor and fell hard up against the wall," was Donna's measured answer, spoken with downcast eyes.

The nurse looked at her with sympathy and a career acquired dose of suspicion. Emergency Nursing was my specialty when I was working, and as seasoned Emergency Room nurses, we had been trained and conditioned to recognize signs of abuse. She took Donna's vital signs and made sure she was stable before directing her to the waiting room.

"What did you tell her?" asked Max, who was now sober enough to realize the magnitude of what he had done.

"I told her I slipped and fell against the wall."

"Good," said Max. "I'm so sorry. I swear to you I will never do that again. Please don't tell them what happened. I know I was wrong."

Donna turned away without answering, leaving him to fret about it while she was in the treatment area being seen by a doctor. Some time passed before the busy Emergency Room had a place for Donna to be examined.

"Here is your gown to change into. It opens down the back," said the nurse who brought her in from the waiting room.

She read the triage nurse's notes and asked Donna what her pain level was on a scale of 0-10, 0 being no pain at all and 10 being the worst she could imagine.

"Eight." She was no stranger to pain, but this hurt.

The nurse nodded. "The doctor will be in shortly. Here is your buzzer to call us if you need something or if your pain gets worse," the nurse, said.

The doctor breezed into the exam room. "Hello, Donna. What happened tonight?"

Donna repeated her bogus story about falling into the wall and was met with the same suspicion as in the triage room. He examined her all over her body and she grimaced when he pushed on her ribs.

"Are you having any trouble breathing?"

"No."

"Okay, I'm going to order an X-ray of your chest and a urinalysis. Radiology should be along shortly to get you," the doctor told her.

Her x-rays completed and urine specimen delivered to the nurse, Donna was left alone with her thoughts and questions. "What happens now? Max was so sincere, and I don't think he will hurt me again. Where would I go with my mom and the boys? How would I be able to take care of myself and them without his help? Would I be better off with him or without him?"

Her thoughts were interrupted by the doctor coming into the exam room.

"I looked at your x-rays and it doesn't look like you have any fractures, but bruised ribs can be just as painful as breaks. Tell me again what happened, honestly."

Donna froze. The word "honestly" hung over her like a menacing black cloud.

"I slipped on some water and fell hard against the wall," she repeated.

"Now I will be honest with you. These bruises look too big and dark to have been caused by a slip and fall. Did someone push or throw you against that wall? Who?"

He asked "who" so quickly after the first question that Donna knew he already had the answer. The doctor knew she was lying.

"Be honest with me, Donna. I've been an ER doctor for a long time, and I know someone did this to you. At this time of night, I think it might be a husband or boyfriend. You should not be going back there. It isn't safe. This time it's bruised ribs and maybe a kidney because there was a little blood in your urine. But what about next time? I would like to call the police to come and speak with you."

"No!" Donna said firmly. "No police. This has not happened before," she lied, "and it won't happen again." Donna wanted to go back home with him despite the doctor's concerns.

"I'm disappointed to hear that, Donna, because I'm worried about you, but I can't force you to report him if you don't want to," he said, concern showing in his eyes. "The nurse will be in with your discharge instructions."

The nurse was all business. "Take deep breaths frequently to keep your lungs from collapsing or from getting pneumonia. Rest and take ibuprofen or naproxen for pain. Apply ice, then heat to the bruised areas, watch for obvious blood in your urine, and follow up with your doctor." The nurse recited the instructions and discharged her to the care of her husband, her abuser.

From the corner of her eye, Donna saw the doctor and nurse sadly shake their heads. On the way home in the car, Donna silently prayed that Max would get the help he needed.

The next day, she felt sore all over and some bruises were starting to appear on her arms. The boys noticed, and she had to tell them what happened.

"Mom, this has gone far enough," George said. "We need to put a stop to it. He's going to really hurt you one day. It wasn't long ago he gave you two black eyes, and now this."

Donna felt hopeless and helpless. "What are the options? I need him. I can't take care of your grandmother and your little brother physically or financially without him. I'll be okay."

"No, Mom, you won't. Are you forgetting what you saw on his computer? 'How to kill someone quickly without leaving a trace' and the links to poisons? Didn't the doctors suspect poisoning when you were sick and getting worse all the time last month? They even found some chemical in your bloodwork that would have been lethal in larger amounts, but they couldn't prove anything. He's sick, and he's smart. If he wants to hurt you, he'll find a way."

Donna knew they were right. "There is nothing I can do," she said.

"Yes, there is," said Josh quietly, sharing a knowing look with George. "A friend of ours gave us the name of someone here in New Jersey who could, um, take care of the problem, and he wouldn't be able to hurt you, anymore."

Donna felt whatever color was left in her pale face drain out.

"A hitman?" she whispered. She could barely even bring herself to say the words let alone agree to the plan. "No, no, that's not the answer! No!"

"Mom, it's either going to be him or you. You know that. No one will find out; our man will make sure of that. No one would even question it if you told them he took off in a drunken rage and never came back," Josh suggested.

"No, no, no, I can't agree to that. Murder? No. And I can't have you two going to jail for the rest of your lives, or worse." Donna's voice was quivering as she spoke.

"If you won't let us do this, then you have to promise us you will see a lawyer in the morning," said George, "and if he does this again, we won't ask for your permission before we call this guy."

"If it means you two won't do anything stupid and throw your lives away, I'll call him."

This dramatic wake-up call gave Donna the strength to see a lawyer the next day and she started to file the divorce papers. Included with the papers was a handwritten will expressly requesting that, in the event of Donna's untimely death, custody of Alex should not be given to Max, citing his abusive nature and cocaine use. It was clear that Donna feared for her life. But when the time came for her to sign the papers, she couldn't do it.

"You did what?" Josh said, when she told him she changed her mind a few days later. "You stopped the divorce? Why? You promised us you would do it." Josh was beside himself with frustration and worry.

"I know, but I just can't. I don't know why, but I still love him, and I can't take on all these responsibilities without his help, financially or physically. Besides, I can't afford the lawyer. Max controls all the money. He even closed out my credit card accounts. I have no way to pay a lawyer. I know you don't understand this, but Max needs me, and I need him. I'll be okay." Donna wasn't sure she believed that, but she felt she had to say it. "He swears he will go to AA and get better. He's not like that when he's sober."

"And how often is that?"

Silence was her answer. Donna knew her sons were right, but she felt trapped in a stunning, ornate cell from which there was no escape. There was no way out of this prison. She felt alone and totally isolated, like a caged animal in the zoo that was her home.

# Chapter 10

Just Leave!

It's easy to judge women in abusive situations. It's hard for someone not in that situation to imagine why someone would stay in a place where they are in danger.

*"Just get out."*

*"Leave!"*

*"He's going to hurt you."*

*"Aren't you afraid he will hurt the kids?"*

*"Why do you let him treat you like that?"*

*"Call the cops; they'll help you."*

Before you judge, consider what might be going on that is preventing her from leaving. It's not always black and white. We don't have the ability to gaze into a person's heart, soul, mind, or home without an invitation. She has probably had experiences that we will, hopefully, never need to encounter, and that makes the situation complex.

Imagine that the victim is you, and you had to deal with one or more of these awful scenarios. Did the abuser threaten your life if you left? Did he take away your source of income? Did he threaten to take away your children? Did he take away your car keys? Did he threaten the lives of your children or even your pets? Did he threaten to convince the police that you are the abuser? Did he bug your house? Did he threaten to spread vicious rumors to your family, friends, or on social media platforms? Is he trying to turn your children against you? Did he threaten to find you wherever you go? Would you be able to support yourself and your children if you left him and put him in jail? Do you need physical help such as for an illness that you would lose if you left? Is your abuser a "pillar of the community" and you fear no one will believe you?

Now consider how easy, or hard, it would be for you to leave or get away if these were the things with which you had to deal. I expect for most of us it would be no easy task. It isn't for victims, either. For many victimized survivors the fear is real. Threats of physical injuries to oneself, a family member, or even a pet, can be the glue that binds people to an abusive or unhealthy relationship. Sometimes victims can be terrified of their abusers but almost as terrified to be alone. What if they have no place to go? What about victims who have been staying behind tending hearth and home while their partners work away from home? They may have no employable skills, or they may have been out of the workplace for so long that the thought of returning to it is daunting. How would they make enough money to support themselves and their children? If a victim presses charges and the police arrest the abuser, how would he make money to pay child support or alimony from jail?

Remember, also, that there may have been a lot of good times mingled in with the bad, and it's likely that they do, or did, love each other in some ways, but love must be distinguished from possession. No one is anyone else's property. Even a marriage license does not allow someone to have complete and utter control over a partner, including in bed. It is illegal in all 50 states, to varying degrees, which are based on the offense, for someone to force unwanted sexual activity on a spouse. Being in a committed relationship does not mean entirely relinquishing yourself to another person. Love means respect and compromise, not possession and control. Sometimes victims just don't want to give up whatever good things they have out of fear of the unknown, or maybe just because they don't want to give up those good things at all and are willing to withstand the abuse. Yin and Yang.

Many times, abusers are deviously successful at convincing victims that the blame lies with them, not the perpetrator. This is one reason that people like Donna, who are used to feeling worthless to start with, stay when they should leave. This is manipulative control, and control is not love. If the victim buys these lies, the impetus to leave is virtually nonexistent. She may believe that all she must do is become better herself and not do things that raise the ire of her partner, for the abuse to stop. Maybe she even subconsciously feels she deserves to be hurt. Add guilt and the stage for failure is set.

Even if a survivor is fortunate enough to get out of the situation, those negative messages that had been planted in a victim's brain remain stored in that brain, continuing to govern the survivor's life choices. Hopefully, no new trauma is added to these psychological wounds, but unfortunately, sometimes the person develops a relationship with another abuser. The mindset of a victim can be hard to shake, the little voices can stick around, and if one begins another abusive relationship, the cycle can begin again. Emotional abuse leaves no visible marks on the body, but the scars are there, invisible to the eye but hard at work affecting a survivor's emotions, words and actions, and controlling the person at every step of life.

With Donna, allowing people to control her was a repetitive pattern in her life, due, in no small part, to her dysfunctional childhood, which caused her low self-esteem. Bad situations such as hers can be stubbornly hard to reconcile. People are constantly composing chapters in their lives, the pages of which they may not want to, or cannot, tear out just yet, despite the pain.

More than half of victims do not report abuse for any of the above-mentioned reasons, and feel their only option is to suffer in silence. Sometimes leaving only serves to anger the abuser and escalates his anger and his actions. The World Health Organization calls Domestic Violence a hidden crime and refers to its prevalence in society as an epidemic.[9]  According to the Partnership Against

Domestic Violence, a woman is assaulted every nine seconds in this country.[10] The United States Centers for Disease Control and Prevention says one in four women and one in 10 men will experience either sexual, physical, or psychological intimate partner violence (IPV) in their lifetime.[11] In addition, federal data show that about half of female homicide victims and about 5 % of men are killed by current or past intimate partners.[12] Bringing law enforcement into the picture may be the only way to stop an abuser if the victim is strong enough to enlist them, but sadly, even that is not always a fail-safe solution to ensuring a person's safety. Restraining orders are the best bet available to avoid contact with an abuser, except maybe creating total anonymity, but they are not fool proof.

Sometimes, women like Donna don't leave right away because they are not being physically abused at first. Often, people don't equate verbal degradation as abuse, but it is, and don't be fooled into thinking that it won't get worse. Life situations can change and new triggers to violence that had not been present before can enter the equation. Problems with a child, job loss, increasing financial concerns, or maybe even a car dying can be enough to strike a match that had previously been cold. This doesn't always happen, but it's not uncommon for emotional abuse to escalate to physical or even sexual abuse with new triggers such as the victim trying to escape, as if to say, "If I can't have you, no one else will, either." Your safety comes first, so before you formulate your escape plan, always consider this possibility and add a plan for protection into the mix, even if it means changing your routines.

If you take out a protection from abuse (PFA) order, stick to it yourself. Please curb the urge to meet with your abuser during that time to discuss things or see if there is anything left to your relationship. Should you choose to do this, be aware that you will be risking your safety and even your credibility with law enforcement and others who will look at you as not being serious about helping your own situation. Donna tried four times to get a divorce from Max, but each time she was unsuccessful. He had her financially strapped, threatened her life, and the stress would cause exacerbations of her Lupus, weakening her and reminding her that she would not be able to do it on her own. She couldn't work, wouldn't be able to pay medical bills, and she had her mother to consider. They had no place to go. She was in her own words "terrified" of Max and what he would do to her if she tried to leave. Gina's stake in their home was a consideration as well. If they abandoned him, chances are she would have no way at all to recoup the money she loaned to Max.

No matter how smart or wise we think we are, unless we have been in someone else's shoes, we don't know what we would do. As a Sexual Assault Nurse Examiner (SANE), aka Forensic Nurse Examiner, I was one of two nurses who cared for victims of sexual assault, domestic violence, and child abuse in the Emergency Room in Rocky Mount, North Carolina. SANEs examined victims, collected evidence for law enforcement, and served as expert witnesses in the event the cases went to trial, which, unfortunately, was not often. One patient I had cared for was covered in bruises, which I photographed, documented, and delivered to the police. My patient was less than hopeful about any justice being served. Her husband was "someone." He served the community, and everyone liked him. He was also a wife beater. At that time, the loose bangle bracelets were in style and she had a whole string of them up her arm, almost to her elbow. I admired them until she told me that each time her husband beat her up, she bought a new one. My heart broke and I could feel the anger well up inside. I tried my best to encourage her to get help, and told her where to go to get it, but my words fell on deaf ears. She was terrified of him, and she didn't feel she had any other options but to go right back to the hell hole she left. She went back, the police seemed disinterested, and she was right: nothing was done. I often wonder what happened to that anguished woman. These are shoes in which no one should ever have to walk. My mantra became No More Bracelets. The good news is that, once a person makes the switch from victim to survivor, there is hope that he or she can shed the remnants of negative thoughts that had previously influenced decision-making and replace them with positive ones.

If you look only at all the depressing statistics above, you may feel hopeless, but that isn't true. Despite the roadblocks, there are people who can help you over the hurdles. In Chapter 20 you will find many tips on leaving or surviving in your current situation. Take action! You are worth it. You are a valued person. You deserve not to live in pain and fear. It may not be easy getting out, but it will be worth it. There are plenty of people who find a way to start over with a new perspective on life. You can be one of them. Most places have undisclosed shelters for women and or their children. Unfortunately, shelters for men are rare because there is less of a need for them, but men can still take advantage of other resources for help. (See Chapter 19).

# Chapter 11

Max has a story, too, and it's not one of Sunday dinners and undying love and devotion from his parents. Wealth was the operative word for him, a perfect example of a good thing that went bad. Money opened doors of opportunity for him that were followed by doors leading to the beginning of a dark tunnel with no exit and no U-turns. In a sense, riches to virtual rags, embodied by personal failure.

His father, Phillip, was a very successful businessman, and he and Max's mother, Irene, were often gone, leaving him and his siblings to fend for themselves. They had a maid, a chauffeur and all the independence they wanted thanks to this entitled existence. It was also tantamount to having absentee parents, creating an emotional void and a lack of the bonding that is necessary to develop stable emotional health. His mom was mean and self-absorbed, and his dad was cold and emotionally removed. They both drank heavily, setting a poor standard for their children and providing ample tools for alcoholics-in-training. Even as a pre-teen, Max would raid his parents liquor cabinet, and he became hooked on alcohol at an early age. His parents either didn't realize what was happening or didn't care. Of course, how could they sense that Max was having a problem when they were heavy drinkers, themselves, and rarely present to observe the onset and progression of this disease in their children?

While building a lucrative business, Phillip was also developing a more and more familiar relationship with his secretary. His mom was no saint, either. She was an angry and spiteful woman, and when her cheating husband asked for a divorce and moved out of the house and in with his mistress, she packed up teenagers Max and his brother, Danny, and tossed them out, instructing them to "go and live with your dad and the cunt." (Moniker sound familiar? Be careful what you say in front of your children, parents, they double as parrots when you aren't around.) Donna didn't understand it the time Max hit her, gave her a black eye and screamed "You're just like her!" Who? Later she learned why he, in a rage, transferred the resentment he harbored against his mother onto her, but she still didn't understand how whatever she had done to incur his wrath was anything like what his mother did, and she may not have done anything remotely resembling his mother's behavior. She was probably merely the innocent recipient of uncontrolled anger at another human being against whom that anger could not be directed, a physically expressed transference of anger. Max was not shy about expressing his hatred for his mother, calling her "incredibly self-absorbed." Irene, in turn, blamed Donna for Max's problems, which is characteristic of a narcissistic-like personality such as hers. Narcissists want to blame everyone else for the negative consequences of their own actions. She certainly wasn't going to blame herself for Max's adult shortcomings. It seems like she totally missed the connection between poor parenting and poor adult outcomes. Imagine how you would feel growing up in an entitled environment without love or supervision, having everything you could want but feeling unloved, unwanted, and discarded? Max knew that his anger and resentment was growing as time passed but he was unable to express it in acceptable ways.

I don't want to believe that abusers are born abusers; rather I want to believe that they are created, that they are people who, had they been fortunate enough to enjoy a stable childhood home, may never have laid a hand on another person. I want to believe that many bad people may not have been bad had they been given their own healthy blueprint for success: a strong and loving family. Research bears this out. Certain mutations of the MAOA gene (The Warrior Gene), found on the X chromosome, and the CDH 13 gene have been shown to predispose men (predominantly) to violence, but it is not a foregone conclusion that all men possessing one or both of these genes will resort to violence to handle their anger issues.[13] The genes are present in about 40 % of the population, but obviously, they don't manifest themselves in 40 % of the population, thank goodness. Because women have two X genes, they respond differently to the propensity to violence that the mutated MAOA gene can represent for men. Testosterone levels, which are naturally higher in men, also contribute to the aggression found more in men than women. In genome studies of criminals, it was shown that 10 % of the violent offenders carried these genes while the non-violent offenders had none. [14]

What has come to be widely accepted through much research, however, is that, although genes that may contribute to violent behavior do exist, the most significant factors in whether aggressive behaviors develop or not are environmental. Dr. Jasmin Wertz is a developmental psychologist at Duke University in Durham, North Carolina, where she studies how genetic make-up and environment shape personality and development during childhood. "If you have two people in front of you with exactly the same genetic score, one might go on to commit a crime and the other one won't. It doesn't really give you the information you need to make predictions with any kind of certainty," she states. She and her associates conducted a study with a sampling of adults, assigning them a genetic score based on how much their genetic make-up contributed to positive outcomes or negative behaviors in their lives. Her studies showed that genetic factors accounted for 1% of the difference between whether people went on to commit crimes, as opposed to 3-5% of the difference being due to socioeconomic factors. [15] It would appear, then, that in the game of nature (genetics) versus nurture (environment), nurture offers up the strongest ante. Giving your children a solid, stable background is essential to their success as an adult, whether they carry the so-called Warrior Gene or not. Much of this research supports what is noted in Chapter 4 in terms of childhood trauma leading to aberrant behavior in adults.

Lawyers have already attempted to use the criminal gene theory in their defense of violent offenders, mostly during the sentencing phase of the trial.[16] Heaven help us if our judicial system ever becomes easy on violent offenders. We may not be able to control what genes we pass down to our offspring, but we can do something to prevent the problems that contribute to people finding themselves in the position of the perpetrator of a crime: we can give our children a solid, stable upbringing. Nature and nurture are not exclusive; they are designed to play together as a team, with environment holding the higher card. Treat your children with love and guidance.

Despite parental neglect and unbridled drinking, Max was popular and a successful student and athlete in high school, and he was even awarded a baseball scholarship to Northwestern University, his whole life ahead of him. College is where most young people get a taste of real independence from their parents' rule, but Max had a head start, and displayed his prowess proudly by excelling in Partying 101, graduating from alcohol to drugs. Not unexpectedly, these dubious skills resulted in his failure to finish his college education, one that might even have led to a career in baseball, the sport he loved. After Max flunked out of college, he went to work in his father's prospering real estate business. He managed to make a good living while continuing to drink to excess and do drugs, and eventually met and married a woman who shared his recreational choices. Donna, of course, was not around for this part of Max's life, but she had later gathered information from mutual acquaintances. His first wife, Carol, had family and friends in the New Jersey town in which they lived, but Max allegedly didn't like sharing her attention, and they soon moved to another town, where they continued their perpetual partying. Max was gradually isolating Carol from the people she loved, and at some point, she began to understand who Max really was and became weary of their volatile relationship. Sadly, she, too, was in a downward substance abuse spiral, getting arrested for Driving Under the Influence (DUI), and feeling physically ill. She wanted to get away from him but had no means or resources to do it, so her father contacted a lawyer for her to help her begin divorce proceedings. Meanwhile, Carol's birthday rolled around, and Max wanted to go out to celebrate. Carol felt ill, experiencing severe abdominal pain and difficulty breathing, so instead of going out to eat, they went to a hospital. The drugs and alcohol had caught up with her, and her body had become too weak to fight back against the forces invading it. Her liver was enlarged, and her lungs were infected. On her 34th birthday, instead of celebrating a new year of life and returning home to start over, Carol died of pneumonia within the cold walls of a hospital, leaving Max alone with their six-year old little boy, Carl.

Some of the information about Max's first marriage came from an unexpected source. On Carl's eighteenth birthday the phone rang, and the female caller asked for Carl. He was not available, but in the next few minutes, Donna learned the details of Max's previous life.

The caller was a friend of Carol's, one of several who blamed Max for Carol's death. They were furious with him and wanted to tell Carl who his father really was but wanted to wait until he turned 18. There had even been a time after Carol's death that these friends considered finding a way to gain custody of Carl because they deemed Max an unfit father. There is a good chance they were right, but for whatever reason, that did not happen. In fact, their motives for contacting Carl and whatever other details they were planning to divulge remain a mystery. They apologized to Donna for not sharing this with her before she married Max, leaving her to lament that omission.

According to Donna, she has no knowledge of Max ever striking Carol, but physical assault is only one component of domestic violence. Domestic Violence, or Intimate Partner Violence (IPV), as it is now called, can be in the form of sexual assault or psychological aggression as well as physical aggression. It's not about love. It's about possession, coercion and control fueled often by deep-seated anger. The combination of factors, upbringing and biological, that join forces to create the kind of person who treats others with disdain and disrespect, ruins lives, and not just one or two. They cause a chain reaction wreck involving the abuser and whoever becomes close to him or her. An interesting phenomenon in Max's family portrait is that his younger brother, Danny, the sibling to whom he was the closest, was not like him. They had the same parents and the same life experiences for the most part, but Danny was quieter and exhibited none of the anger that Max did against their mother. It was never obvious how Danny dealt with their dysfunctional childhood existence. Perhaps he had been dealt a different combination of genetic and environmental cards. Perhaps their birth order dictated the roles they played within the family structure. Maybe their contrasting personalities elicited different responses from their parents. Whatever the reason, one thing was certain: they did love each other, and Danny was devoted to his big brother.

Danny ran an insurance agency that, not surprisingly, held the policy covering Max's business.

Max was enjoying a lucrative business but began spending much of the profit on his dangerous habits and mismanaging the rest, resulting in a precarious financial situation.

"Danny, you have to help me, I'm in the red," Max told Danny one day, agitated.

"Again? Come on Max, I can't keep bailing you out like this or I'll be in the red, too."

"No, this would just be a loan. I'm working on a big account. As soon as it comes through, which will be soon, I'll pay you back."

"Max, how do I know all that money won't go up your nose?" Danny countered.

"I swear I'm going straight. I know I messed up, but I'm getting out of that life and I'm going to build this business up to where it should be, I promise you. Please."

"How much do you need?" asked Danny, warily.

"$80,000."

"Max....!"

"I know, it's a lot, but it will be worth it this time."

Danny should have listened to his instincts, brotherly love or not, but, once again, he caved.

"How is the project going, Max?" asked Danny, after more than enough time had elapsed since he dispensed the loan money.

"It fell through, Danny. I'm really sorry." He said it with a respectable amount of manufactured contrition.

"Now what? How are you going to pay me back?" He was frustrated with his brother's irresponsibility.

"I have an idea, but you have to be onboard, and it has to stay between us."

"Max, what are you planning on doing?".

"Just hear me out. This can't fail. We can stage a robbery at the business. We'll get in there and steal some computers and equipment, file a police report, and your insurance company will pay the claim. It won't be any skin off your back if the company pays, and then you'll get your money back."

Max laid out the plan with such scary precision that even Danny had a hard time being skeptical.

"Max, are you serious? Is this what it's come to, just for some blow and booze?"

"No, no. The project fell through, Danny, I swear. I had a big client and he backed out of the sales contract. It would have set me up for good. We know the building, the exits, the alarm system. We can cut the wires so no one will even hear about it until I come in the next day."

As usual, Max's baby brother could not turn him down. The operation went as planned with no one the wiser for it. Twice. Danny had an innate inability to say "no" to Max, be it bailing him out of jail, pulling him out of debt, paying his lawyer's fees, providing alibis for his clandestine activities, and now, even committing felonies. There was no end to Danny's love for his brother.

# Chapter 12

Jekyll and Hyde

Donna describes Max as living inside their home "under a shroud of darkness: angry, spiteful, and resentful." Outside his family he presented a very different face. To his community he was a successful businessman, a football, baseball and soccer coach, and a block captain. She felt he believed this served to normalize an internally troubled, conflicted life. Few who knew him would have guessed there was an alter-ego at play, a Mr. Hyde to his normal Dr. Jekyll, waiting to emerge at the slightest irritating provocation. The police knew but couldn't do anything about it because Donna wouldn't press charges.

When his father sold his real estate business, Max went out on his own and rented a building to start a business selling communication equipment. Ironically, this building was across the street from Donna's first husband's family farm. Donna didn't know if this was simply the best deal and the best facility for Max's needs, or if it was a show of superiority and dominance over Donna's ex.

Donna often went on business trips with Max, and the trip to London, England, was one of them. At the airport, the trip got off to a rocky start.

"I'll be back before the plane leaves. Just wait here," Max told Donna as he got in his car.

"Max, why can't you just stay and wait with me? What if the plane leaves before you get back? At least give me my passport," pleaded Donna.

"You don't need it. I'll be back. Stop being such a whiny bitch, will you?"

Donna watched Max drive off, then went in to get a drink at the specialty coffee shop in the airport while she waited, an iced mocha latte, her favorite. She had enough left in her wallet from her allowance to be able to afford that.

"See, I told you I would get back on time," Max said as the call for boarding the plane was announced over the PA system.

Donna looked at him squarely in the face. She knew.

"Where did you go, Max?" she asked.

"None of your business, you stupid bitch."

"You scored some dope, didn't you, Max?"

"If you must know, I got a few pills to take the edge off of the flight."

"You never have any worries about flying. Why were those necessary to get now and risk missing the plane?"

"Shut your ugly mouth up!" Max said, his voice rising, attracting quizzical looks from strangers. "I'm here now, so let's go before you make me miss the plane and my meeting!"

Donna knew it was no use to argue and was becoming uncomfortable with the attention they were drawing.

They heeded the last call for boarding, heading up the ramp and into the plane to their reserved seats in first class.

"Good afternoon. My name is Allison and I will be your flight attendant for today," said a pretty young woman who had immediately caught Max's eye. "There are a few safety instructions I have to give you and then you can relax and enjoy your flight to London."

Allison had barely finished the instructions than Max was asking for a drink.

"Hey, Doll. Allison, is it? Would you be so kind as to bring me a whiskey and water?"

"Certainly, Sir. I'll bring it right out."

Allison had brought three drinks out for Max and by that time Donna was becoming concerned.

"Max, I think you've had enough drinks," Donna whispered quietly.

"You're so stupid. You don't know what you're talking about," growled Max. "Allison, another whisky and water here."

The flight attendant reluctantly complied with his request, watching him warily.

"See? I'm fine. She wouldn't have given me another drink if I wasn't," Max gloated to Donna.

"Well, make that one your last," Donna advised him, then whispered "Drugs and alcohol are not a good match."

"I'm fine!" Max said, his voice rising. "And I don't have to listen to you! You're just a dumb broad and you don't know what you are talking about! I'll drink as much as I want!"

It was clear that Max was losing control. Even the passengers in coach were straining their necks to see what was going on up front.

"Hey, Doll," Max slurred, more sweetly now, to Allison, who had been watching and listening closely. "How about a shot of whiskey?"

"I'm sorry, sir, I can't give you anymore," she said.

"What do you mean you can't give me anymore!?" said Max loudly, becoming visibly agitated. "I'm a paying customer, and I'm not driving, so you can't deny me."

"Sir," said Allison, calmly but firmly, "you may not realize it, but the cabin pressure in an airplane is a little lower than the outside, making your body more susceptible to the effects of alcohol, and I don't think you should have anymore right now."

"Max, let it alone. You're embarrassing both of us," said Donna, trying to defuse this volatile situation.

"Shut up, Bitch, if you know what's good for you!" Max yelled at her.

By this time, a few men were perched on the edges of their seats, anticipating the need to help subdue this man.

"I want another drink and it's your job to give it to me!" Now he was yelling at Allison, who stood firm.

"Sir, I will not give you any more alcohol, and if you continue to act in this manner, I will have Scotland Yard waiting for you when we land."

The passengers clapped, nodding their approval of the flight attendant's handling of this disturbing situation. That seemed to wake Max up and he settled down, grumbling about the terrible service and threatening to file a complaint against the airlines. Allison wasn't worried about that. She had plenty of witnesses to his combative behavior. Donna lowered her head in shame, earning her looks of sympathy from passengers. When the plane landed, she woke him up from his drug and alcohol-induced stupor to disembark, then guided him to the luggage claim, where they hastily retrieved their belongings and headed to the hotel, where Max would sleep it off. The next morning, true to form, Max was duly repentant, seducing Donna with his immense charm leading to a morning of passion.

Once home, Max was quiet for the next few days while he tended to work details and Donna had a bit of a reprieve from fear, but it didn't last long. Soon, all the old behaviors resurfaced.

"Where did you go, today, Donna? What did you do?" Max eyed Donna suspiciously. "You put 50 miles on the car since yesterday."

"What, now you're checking the odometer on the car? Seriously, Max. What is your problem?" answered Donna.

"YOU! You're my problem!" screamed Max. "I can't trust you, that's why I check the odometer!"

"What do you think I'm going to do? I went grocery shopping and picked up something from the pharmacy for Marcy. She's sick. How could I do anything else, Max? I don't have any money. You closed my checking account!"

"Yes, and your credit cards, too. I'll give you money when you need it, but now I'll know where it goes. What did you get at the grocery store? Probably all the wrong things again, as usual." Max was looking through the kitchen cabinets and pacing around the kitchen with a mug of coffee as he ranted. Donna wondered if he had just downed some pills or if he needed some. Sometimes she couldn't tell. He wasn't drunk yet. That would come next.

"And what were you saying to your little friend, Marcy? Complaining again? That's all you ever do is complain. I don't know why I keep you around sometimes. You're just plain lazy and stupid."

Max noticed the pile of dirty laundry in the hallway and stopped to stare at it. "And I suppose that's why this laundry isn't done, right, because you were helping your friend? What about me, Donna? You're always willing to help your delinquent sons and your friends, but me, I don't count. I need shirts!"

Donna froze in her tracks, terrified of what would be coming next. "I'll have them washed and ironed for you by tomorrow morning. I have plenty of time."

"Well, you better start right now, or you won't be able to get this off of everything," he said as he proceeded to pour his coffee all over the pile of clothes. "That should keep you from talking on the phone all night. And stay away from Marcy. You don't need to be bringing her germs home to everyone. I can't afford to get sick."

Donna scurried around as quickly as she could to get the clothes sprayed with a laundry pre-washing spray before the stains had a chance to set, and then she threw them quickly into the washer.

"I better not see a stain or a wrinkle on those shirts tomorrow," he scolded.

Everything always had to be perfect for Max. Not a wrinkle on his clothes, not a piece of furniture that wouldn't pass the white glove test, the exact groceries he wanted, meals prepared precisely the way he wanted them, nothing out of place. Donna did her best, even when she wasn't feeling well, to make sure Max had no reason to be upset about anything. It didn't always work.

Donna had Max's shirts pressed and food on the table the next morning by the time he woke up. Without comment, he ate his breakfast and left. Donna sat down with a cup of coffee and sighed. She took a *Vanity Fair* magazine out of its hiding place and flipped through the pages. She had to be careful that Max didn't see her stash because that's another thing he complained about: she read too many magazines. After she had finished reading, she disposed of it immediately and went about her daily routine, making sure there was enough, and the right kind, of food in the house; that there were exactly the right number of pillows on the bed and sofa; that the liquor cabinet was stocked; that all the dry cleaning was picked up; that all the clothing was folded exactly right and put away. She paid special attention to his socks, because if he couldn't find a matched pair, he would open the drawer and spill its entire contents all over the floor for her to pick up and put back. Then she checked the boys' rooms to make sure they had all their own toiletries and their clothes were picked up. She didn't want to relive the chaos that erupted when one of them borrowed his shampoo, or the day he threw their clothes outside because they weren't picked up. While she was cleaning hers and Max's room, she noticed that her diamond ring was missing, and she was furious. Max was the only one who knew where she kept it. What he didn't know was that the ring was a treasured heirloom of Gina's that she had gotten from Mario, and when Donna told her about it, that Di Orio temper showed up. Gina stormed into his office demanding her ring back. Fortunately, he hadn't sold it yet, and he complied. It seemed there was no messing with Gina Di Orio.

This was not the first time Max had stolen from Donna. She had plenty of "I'm sorry" jewelry around that he had bought her, so she supposed he didn't look at it as stealing since they were gifts from him. Once he even sold some of it, then took her credit card, while it was still active, to pay off his income taxes. She didn't even bother to try to get a confession out of him. That would be emotional suicide. The day after the ring incident, Donna had just laid down to take a nap after her morning chores were finished and the doorbell rang. She got up to answer and she was greeted by a deliveryman with a huge bouquet of sweet-smelling roses accented by sprigs of baby's breath and feathery ferns with a large yellow bow to adorn it. All the card said was "I'm sorry." She thanked the man, sniffed the flowers, set them on the table and went back to bed.

This persistent pattern of abuse, remorse, repentance, and shows of affection are what kept Donna, and what keeps so many other women, from leaving an unhealthy relationship. They want so badly to be loved and feel wanted by someone that even a morsel of positive attention is enough to keep them there. Since Donna always felt like the problems in their relationship were her fault, and Max continually fed her low level of self-esteem with his insults, she took whatever sprinkles of attention he would show her as signs of his love, instead of control. She believed him when he told her it was her fault that he was the way he was, which he did often. It's always about them, the master manipulators.

"The vice president of my company called Danny today," Max told Donna one day as they were driving home from the mall where they had shopped for some new clothes.

"What did he want?" Donna was surprised he had even shared that with her.

"He said the business wasn't doing well and that Danny needed to do something about it. He shouldn't have done that. He should have called me if there was a problem."

"Well, Max, maybe you are the problem. Maybe that's why he called Danny instead of you," Donna offered slowly, watching him as she spoke. His face was getting red, which was not a good sign, but he controlled himself. Donna wasn't worried. They were in the car; what could he do to her?

"I need $50,000 to keep the business afloat but I can't get a loan unless someone cosigns for it. I told them you would do that," Max said.

"No, Max, I won't help bail you out this time. I'm not Danny. Where would I get $50,000 if you default on the loan? You don't have a good track record with loans. We might even lose the house. I can't do it."

By now Max's face had turned a crimson red and he slammed on the brakes so hard that Donna lurched forward and hit her head on the steering wheel. The car behind them honked the horn loudly and she heard the brakes squeal as it barely missed rear-ending them. "Max! What did you do that for? There was no reason to stop! You almost made the car behind us hit us!" Donna was rubbing her head and neck and trying to fight off the dizziness and nausea she was feeling from the head injury. Max just stared straight ahead as they rode the rest of the way home in silence.

Fortunately, Donna didn't need to go to the hospital that time. She was sore for a few days after that but just took some over the counter pain medicine and some muscle relaxers she had left over from her back pain. After she refused to co-sign for Max's loan, they started looking around for locations to move the business that did not come with as high a price tag for rent as the current place in New Jersey. They looked around in Pennsylvania but ultimately found a suitable place in New Jersey, anyway. Donna really isn't sure why, but he did move his business around a lot, even when it was good. For most people, financial straits would be a wake-up call to straighten up, but for addicts, straightening up is not just a matter of resolve. Max couldn't stop himself on his path to self-destruction.

Acts of desperation are not uncommon for addicts as they struggle to support their habits, and domestic abuse is more prevalent among alcoholics and drug abusers as they struggle to control the only thing they can in their lives, their weaker partners. Max would steal Donna's money, her active credit cards or her valuables to get his fixes. When he was angry at her for something, tangible or not, he would close the credit cards down or stomp on her jewelry as punishment. Once he reported his own credit card stolen and accused Donna of being the thief. She had to answer to law enforcement before they finally cleared her. He would shut her phone down and throw out mementos that were important to her. For the most part, when Max was sober, he could contain himself, and during those times he was able to acknowledge that what he was doing was wrong. He usually remembered what he had done after the fact, but when the chemicals he was ingesting took over his brain, they controlled him, and he was no longer capable of making rational choices in behavior.

# Chapter 13

Fantasies for Survival

The holidays were approaching, and Donna had planned a beautiful family dinner for Thanksgiving complete with all the festive decorations and holiday food. It was hard to get everyone together anymore, since they were all going in different directions. Alex was still in single digits while the three older boys were in their late teens. She was happy to be having everyone together at the same time. Unfortunately, Max was high when he got to the table, but they managed to have a nice, uneventful family meal. Donna was exhausted but it was a good exhausted.

"Hey, Donna," Max said, after everyone had gone. "Come over here. I have something for us to loosen up a little bit. You're all stressed out."

Max had laid out the familiar tray with white powder and a straw on the coffee table. Alongside was a glass of cognac, one of Max's favorites.

"Max, I'm not doing that with you, anymore. You know that. Besides, I'm tired. I've been working all day on the dinner and I just want to go to bed. And you don't need to be doing that, either, especially with a cognac booster."

"Oh, so you are little Miss Saint, now, are you? Too good for a little coke? You need something to unwind. You're all wound up."

"No, I don't want to do it," Donna insisted.

"What is your problem, Bitch?" Max was becoming more and more agitated. "You spent the whole day making food and fussing over the boys and now you have no time to spend with me! Who gave you the money to buy all that food, or any of the stuff you have here?! All the fancy potted plants and china and silver we used? Who made it possible for you to have all this?! Me! You would be nothing without me and you never even want to do anything with me; it's all the kids!"

Max's face was flushed, and he was pacing around the room. He was so angry that Donna was sure he was going to hit her.

"What do you need these for? They're stupid, just like you!" With that, Max proceeded to dump the potted plants all over the carpeted floor and grind the dirt in with his heels with a vengeance. "These are worthless, too! Why do you need pictures? You see everyone enough!"

Donna had gotten some pictures out for everyone to look at after dinner and Max, in his rage, ripped them into pieces and threw them on the floor with the dirt. "There, that will give you something to do for a while!" He went upstairs. A short time later, he came down with a suitcase and left, slamming the door fiercely behind him. Donna was relieved he was gone but worried, as she always did, that he would cause an accident that would hurt or kill him or other, innocent, people.

She was just relieved that he was able to get through the meal without ruining it. She recalled when Max was unhappy with her cooking and would toss the food at the wall and window. At least she wouldn't have to clean them tonight.

Sometimes Max would take 8-year old Alex along with him on errands, but when Donna learned he took one of these errand runs to pick up his coke, she put her foot down. Donna knew that Max didn't let Alex use the coke, but just exposing him to the scene was negligent. As we all know, children mimic their parents. She could at least not let Max introduce Alex to the path of no return on which he, himself, was traveling. Max would get furious with Donna at first for trying to stop him from taking Alex along out with him, but he settled down, and Donna thinks he knew it was wrong.

Winter and spring came and went, and then the weather was beautiful and the sun warm. Donna, Max, and young Alex headed to their country club pool for some relaxation. A lady sat by the poolside, reading a book and smiling as she watched her family splashing around, laughing and throwing each other in the pool. She rocked that bikini for a woman with four children, all beautiful towheads. Poolside cocktail in hand, she faked annoyance at her hunky husband, skin bronzed from the sun, when he playfully splashed her. They were all yelling for her to come in and join the fun, mischievously lying: "The water's nice and warm!"

Donna smiled, fantasizing where the public playfulness would lead "Barbie and Ken" once the children were all safely tucked in bed and sound asleep. She could only imagine, and she did. She imagined dusty-rose colored silk sheets on a king-sized bed with a canopy shading the bed so just enough light came through to be romantic. Fresh, fragrant flowers sat on the lady's bedside stand with a note that said, "I love you." He undressed and waited for her under the silky sheets. In a few minutes she emerged from her dressing area, a deep cut but flowing lavender nightgown, that was made for anything but sleeping, adorning her perfect body. She slid into bed next to him, and they shared a smile.

"Mom!" This time it was her son who interrupted her fantasy. He motioned towards his dad, who was at the swim-up bar, already on his second vodka and soda and it was only 11:30 in the morning. Donna shook her head and shrugged. It would be futile and potentially incendiary for her to intervene in this phase of Max's self-destruction. Max caught the non-verbal communication between his wife and son and immediately deflected it.

"Don't be such a fag sitting there with your Mama! Get the hell in the pool and make a friend!"

Max's booming voice caught the attention of all the pool-goers and Alex jumped into the water to avoid anyone noticing the tears flowing down his face, which was flushed with embarrassment. Two boys had noticed this interaction and swam over to Alex, asking his name. Donna was relieved to believe that there was still some good left in the world.

"And you! I hope you get a tan or something. You're pasty white!" he yelled to Donna.

She pretended not to hear and buried her head in her Danielle Steele book, refraining from engaging in conversation with Max. This was supposed to be a family day where they could relax and have fun. If only the pool didn't have that swim-up bar. Max wanted to bond with his son, but Alex was shying away from him today, embarrassed by his loud, abrasive voice. They enjoyed pitching and catching ball together in the back yard, but when Alex started getting a little older, he wanted to be with his friends more than his father. This made Max feel rejected and angry, but Alex liked to go to his friends' house so he wouldn't have to see his father drunk and hear him screaming at his mother.

By the time they went home, Max had had his fill at the poolside bar. Donna wanted to drive but giving up his keys to another person, especially her, was out of the question. He drove home drunk and stumbled up the steps and into bed. She sat on the bed, mentally planning her grocery trip. She was feeling low and chose a nice pair of capris and a flowing blouse to wear. They may not have been grocery attire, but they made her feel good about herself. Then, thinking better of it, she hung them back up and slipped on a pair of casual shorts and a nice T-shirt. Numbly, she walked in the store and grabbed a shopping cart. People were beginning to leave work so the store was getting busy, but she couldn't help but notice a beautiful, classy, perfectly coiffed and manicured shopper in the organic food section, placing some fresh arugula in a plastic bag as she chatted on her phone, laughing and smiling. Donna's phone was ringing, too, but she ignored it as she continued to focus on this women, who smiled and said "I love you, too," as she hung up the phone, resuming her inspection of the local produce. Donna finally picked up her phone.

"How much fucking longer are you going to be at the grocery store? I'm hungry," said Max as Donna cleared her mind of her latest thoughts. "Are you really at the grocery store or are you out fucking someone? You thought I was sleeping, but I saw the clothes you were thinking about wearing to go out. What changed your mind? Would that make it too obvious that you weren't going grocery shopping!"

"Max, yes, I am grocery shopping. It was getting late when we got back from the pool and now people are starting to get off work, so the store is busy."

"You can't do anything right. Why did you wait so long to buy groceries? You should have done it yesterday. You better get the right things this time. Don't screw up."

Donna assured him she wouldn't screw up and hung up her phone. She saw Arugula Lady again as she pushed her cart up and down the aisles. She was chatting and laughing with a friend as if she had not a care or timetable in the world. Donna was sure *her* husband would not complain about the contents of her grocery cart.

We all have defense mechanisms to try and keep at bay the silent demons in our subconscious, or conscious, that affect our lives and who we are. Donna is a sensitive and intuitive individual, making her more vulnerable to unseen forces that affected her. Fantasies were one tool she utilized to control painful truths in her life. Fantasies can trigger creativity, help a person better understand him or herself, and even help someone set goals for the future. Some fantasies can be pathologic, indicating mental illnesses such as schizophrenia or delusional disorder, but most are harmless, and those indicative of things that could possibly happen can be productive, such as dreaming of an attainable new career or creative endeavor. Donna's fantasies removed her from reality and protected her from pain for those brief moments.[17] Even though they served a purpose, they couldn't shield her from the gravity of her situation. I can't say that victims and their abusers don't love each other in any way. The good times, even if they are dramatically outweighed by the bad ones, can be enough to sustain someone who craves love, despite the detrimental effect that relationship may be having on the person and those around her. Someone once told me that if a relationship begins to cause a person more pain than pleasure, it's time to break it off. For the average relationship, I believe there is much truth to that thought, but for someone in an abusive relationship, it's an entirely different mental dynamic. Change is hard, and some people are better than others in dealing with it. It's not unlike what Donna felt when her father passed away. He was more of a source of pain than pleasure, but there were good things in their relationship, like his visitations after he left Gina. Bringing gifts was the way Mario showed his love. He was a part of her life and she was a part of his life before he left them, and so it was with Max.

# Chapter 14

Demons in the Lead

Occasionally, Donna's father's doctor's words would echo in her mind: "Gina, if Mario doesn't stop his drinking and smoking, it will kill him," because she knew the same could be true of Max. She tried to tell him, but he wouldn't listen and just said she was dumb and didn't know what she was talking about, usually followed by a "You can't tell me what to do" for good measure. Max was exercising at home when the pain hit.

"Donna, come over here. I think I'm having a heart attack," Max called to her. "I'm having trouble breathing, my chest hurts, my heart is racing, and I'm getting dizzy."

"Go lie down," Donna directed. "I'll call 911 "

Within minutes the mournful wail of sirens and the sight of flashing blue and red lights announced the urgency of their mission. Chills ran up and down her spine as she recalled the time an emergency vehicle arrived at her house for her Nonno, and she was filled with a sense of sadness and dread.

"What symptoms are you having, Mr. Miflin? When did they start? On a scale of 0-10 with 0 being no pain at all and 10 being the worst you can imagine, what number is your pain? Do you have any cardiac history or any other medical history? What were you doing when your symptoms started?" a paramedic asked him.

Emboldened by Max's current state of vulnerability, she gave the paramedics some helpful information.

"He was exercising and snorting coke, that's what he was doing," she informed them.

"Do you use drugs often? How about alcohol?" one of them asked, trying to get a complete history.

"You bitch, Donna. That's none of their business and you had no right to tell them about that," growled Max, throwing her a look that could kill.

"Actually, Mr. Miflin, it is our business to get a complete medical history, and drug use is a very important piece of information. Drugs and alcohol can have devastating effects on your heart. We are not the police, and we are not allowed to report the drug use of our patients to law enforcement. We're only here to help you, not get you in trouble."

"You're lucky, Donna. But you were probably hoping to get me in trouble, weren't you? "I'm starting to get dizzier and sweatier. Can't you do something?" he barked at the paramedics.

They hooked Max up to the portable cardiac monitor. Ventricular tachycardia, a rapid, pre-lethal cardiac arrhythmia stared at them from the screen.

"Mr. Miflin, we are going to give you a strong medication to try to slow down your heart. It's going way too fast and the beats are originating from the bottom of your heart instead of the top, where they should. We may have to shock your heart if the medicine doesn't help."

Swiftly and adeptly the paramedic team inserted an intravenous line into a vein on his hand and pushed the lidocaine in slowly. At the same time, another paramedic was preparing a lidocaine drip, a bag consisting of a 5 % dextrose solution to which lidocaine had been added. This way he would get a loading dose first and then a continual drip to follow to maintain the proper rhythm. They watched him and his monitor closely as neither were getting better. As Max slipped into unconsciousness, the paramedics attached white pads to Max's chest, one on his upper left and one on his lower right chest to the side, and placed a nasal cannula to deliver oxygen from a tank they had brought into the house. The increasingly high pitch of the defibrillator squealed as they set it to shock for ventricular tachycardia, different than the procedure they use for the lethal ventricular fibrillation. Simultaneously placing the paddles on the white pads on Max's chest and looking around to see if anyone was near them or the bed, the paramedic yelled "All clear! Everyone clear!" No sooner were the words out of his mouth than Donna heard the electric click of the paddles, heard a moan from Max and saw his body jump a little off the bed. Immediately Max's heart returned to its normal rhythm. Color began to return to his face, his pulse was stronger, and he started to talk, mostly complaining about what they did to him.

"Thank you so much," said Donna to the team of workers.

"You're welcome, Ma'am. We have him stabilized but we still have to take him to the hospital so they can work him up and find out what happened here today."

"I do not want to go to the hospital," Max said adamantly. "You fixed me. I don't need to go. I'm fine."

"Sir, what we did was a band aid. Ventricular tachycardia is a serious cardiac arrhythmia that leads to ventricular fibrillation, which is cardiac arrest, or sudden death, if not treated. They need to find out what caused this to happen to you, so it doesn't happen again. I'm sorry, but we will need to take you."

Feeling weak, Max let them take him to the hospital. He was admitted and tests were in progress, but before they could complete their assessment, he signed himself out. They knew he wanted to go out for a fix, and they also knew that his drug use was the reason behind his heart problems, but, because they couldn't prove that he would be a danger to himself or others, by law, they couldn't force him to stay. Compliance was not Max's middle name, but he did follow up with his private physician within the next day or two. His 15-minute overall exam found his vital signs to be stable and lungs clear. He denied having any recurrence of the symptoms that precipitated his hospital visit. Since he had signed himself out

Against Medical Advice, or AMA, Donna wanted the doctor to readmit him for observation, but Max would have none of that and the doctor didn't support Donna's wishes. He knew Max's problem and did his duty of encouraging him, but he knew Max's compliance wouldn't last and his problem couldn't be solved in an overnight hospital stay. Complicating his exam was the fact that the doctor had not received Max's medical records from the hospital yet. He talked with him about going through rehab, gave him resource material, and advised Donna to check the places out and verify coverage for services with his insurance carrier. He told Max, in no uncertain terms, that he needed to get clean or he would eventually pay with his life. "De'ja vu," thought Donna, but she was glad for the tough love from the doctor this time.

Max did try to take it easy after that, but he was not in control of himself. His demons charged up right next to him demanding to be heard, and he listened. First his vodka, then he popped a few pain pills he had stashed away, and when that wasn't enough, he went out to find some of the white poison powder. It was only cocaine, he told himself and Donna, but don't let that fool you. Cocaine is a devil and will rob you of your soul.

Two days after Max had seen the doctor, Donna had his breakfast waiting at the table, as she did every morning. He seemed a little wobbly coming down the stairs but nothing more than usual when coming off a bender. She noticed his voice was a bit slurred but again, she was used to that.

"I have a headache," Max said slowly, "and why can't I talk right?"

"Probably because you're not down off of your drunken high yet," Donna said, not even looking at him.

"No, this is different," he said. "I have never had a headache this bad in my life."

As she walked out to the kitchen, she heard a fork drop and then a thump.

"Help me up," Max slurred. "I dropped my fork and when I tried to pick it up, I fell off the chair."

Donna told him to put his arms around her neck so he could assist her as she tried to pull him up. His muscular weight was no match for hers. He put his strong right arm up over her left shoulder, but she stopped short as she realized she felt nothing on her right shoulder. Dismayed, she saw his limp left arm hanging by his side. She looked at his pale face and noticed the left droop and the terror in his eyes. Max had had a stroke.

"Max, can you talk to me?" she said quietly.

Try as he might, all Max could manage was an incoherent mumble. Donna carefully lowered Max to the floor, placed a pillow under his head, covered him with a throw they had draped across the back of the sofa, and called 911.

Once again, the ear-piercing sound of sirens filled the air. Nosy neighbors peeked through curtains or brazenly came out onto their front porches to watch the medical drama unfold as paramedics wheeled Max into the ambulance and whisked him off to the hospital, Donna following behind in their Benz.

As had happened several times in the past, Donna was filled with conflicting thoughts and emotions as she absentmindedly flipped through an old issue of *Time Magazine* that she had found on a table in the Emergency Room waiting room. He might die. Would she feel remorse, sadness, relief, guilt? Or worse, what if he lived but couldn't really live? She didn't know how she would take care of him. Maybe he would need a nursing home. Her thoughts were periodically broken by the sounds of babies and toddlers crying, families and friends disagreeing about one thing or another or people complaining to staff about the long wait. She could smell the nauseating exhaust fumes of ambulances coming in through the emergency vehicle bays and felt like vomiting. "What next?" she thought to herself with a sigh.

"Mrs. Miflin?"

A nurse was standing in front of her.

"You can come back now. The doctor would like to talk to you."

They walked past busy doctors and nurses and came to a room where an obvious code blue was in progress. Her heart skipped a beat but settled down as they bypassed that room and walked on. Donna felt like she was part of a movie being run in slow motion and was grateful when they finally reached Max's room. He looked at her with the same terror in his eyes, still unable to talk, a tear coming down his face. His heart monitor beeped out a steady rhythm and the oxygen coming from a wall unit hissed as it went into the nasal cannula in Max's nose. The fluid in the IV dripped slowly into the connecting plastic tube and was going into a vein in Max's hand. She smelled urine and realized that Max must have lost control of his bladder before they inserted the Foley catheter that was now in his penis and connected to a bag hanging on the stretcher. The nurses had propped his useless arm up on a pillow to prevent swelling of that hand. Donna had never seen him so vulnerable. But she was tired of hospitals. She was tired of all the unpleasant sights, sounds and smells, tired of the trauma that always brought them to one, and tired of the bad news that almost always accompanied visits to the ER.

"Hello, Mrs. Miflin," said Dr. Jones as he pushed aside the curtain separating them from the central nurses' area. "It seems your husband has had a stroke. Since you got him here right away, there is a chance that we can reverse the effects of the stroke, depending on what kind of stroke it is. A stroke is similar to a heart attack but instead of the heart muscle that gets damaged, it's the brain. They can be caused by blood clots, air emboli, or brain bleeds. They can all cause the same symptoms, so in order for us to try to determine what caused his stroke, we did a CT scan of his brain. When strokes are caused by a blood clot, there is a medication that can be given through a vein that will break up the clot, a "clot buster," if you will. If the stroke is caused by a brain bleed, we would make matters worse by giving him this medication. Max's scan showed that his stroke came from a blood clot, but we do not give the clot-buster, tissue plasminogen activator, or tPA, here, so we will be transferring him immediately to a hospital in New York that does it. It's time sensitive, meaning it must be given within three hours of the onset of symptoms, four and a half at the most. Fortunately, the hospital is not far away, even though it's in New York. I'll call ahead so they will be ready for you when you arrive. It is a detailed and risky procedure, but they have had excellent results. If you agree, we'll get the ball rolling for his transfer right away."

Donna didn't have to think twice to give her approval; there was no time to waste.

While Donna was waiting for the ambulance, she checked out the hotels in the hospital area and made a reservation for herself for the night. She called the kids to make them aware of what was going on and then went back to be with Max while they waited, but it wasn't long. The urgency of the situation brought an ambulance almost immediately and before she knew it, they were on the road to another hospital. Even though it wasn't yet noon, Donna was exhausted and drove carefully to New York, a large cup of fast food coffee beside her in the cup holder. No time for Starbucks this time. The minute she arrived, the staff handed her a form with lots of questions about the event and his health history, as well as a consent form giving them permission to administer tPA. As the attending doctor read the forms, a tell-tale, undisguised look of disgust made it clear to Donna when he had reached the part about Max's drug use, the ventricular tachycardia and him signing himself out of the hospital. Despite his obvious distaste for the situation, the doctor completed the process and upheld that part of the Hippocratic Oath recited by medical students everywhere that states "*primum non nocere,*" or "first do no harm." Max was wheeled to the Radiology Invasive Procedures lab and another wait commenced for Donna.

# Chapter 15

Drugs and Alcohol Manifest Themselves

Slumped in another waiting room chair, Donna wanted to take a nap, but the caffeine had something else to say about that. Taking out the journal she kept close by her, she began to fill the next page with the events of the day, her thoughts, and her feelings about it all. An article highlighted on the cover of a *Bon Appetit* that was lying on the end table caught her eye, so she finished her last journal entry and picked up the magazine. "I'll bet Max would like this," she found herself musing. She surprised herself with that futuristic thought given the critical life and death situation Max was facing. At this moment, all she could remember were the good times: the love, the flowers, and the fun, because they had been there. They were the early times, the honeymoon phase of their relationship, before the abuse started, and that had been scattered among the pain. Those times may have been overshadowed by the bad, but they had existed on some level, and when the gravity of the day finally sunk in, she began to cry, despite her effort to control it.

"Mrs. Miflin, the procedure is over, and Max did well. We're going to keep him in the Intensive Care Unit for a few days just to be sure he is out of the woods for complications."

Donna nodded and thanked the doctor giving her the reassuring news. The procedure had worked. The tPA broke up the clot and restored blood flow to Max's brain. Fortunately, it hadn't been without oxygen long enough to cause permanent damage, so within a few days he was back to normal. Donna stayed in the hotel room until Max was moved out of ICU into the Stepdown unit, where he was still on a cardiac monitor, but otherwise treated much like he would have been on a general medical floor. She was glad to be back home in her own bed in her own home in New Jersey, where she finally was able to enjoy some well-deserved and well-needed rest.

Unfortunately, that respite period was short-lived thanks to a midnight phone call from the hospital that Max was in cardiac arrest. Awakened from a deep sleep, Donna was shocked and flustered. Even though she knew that sudden death was a risk they watched out for, it was not something she had consciously anticipated. She hastily threw some clothes on and jumped in her car, keeping a close eye on the speedometer as she drove. If she got caught speeding, the time it would save her getting to the hospital in New York would be eaten up by a police stop. She had no idea what kind of news would be greeting her, and she arrived at the hospital trembling and weak with worry.

"Mrs. Miflin, Max's heart stopped tonight, but we were able to start it beating again. He has a tube in his lungs to help him breathe and his breathing is being controlled by a machine, a ventilator, right now. Once he becomes stable, we'll wean him off the ventilator and decide on a plan going forward. He's back in the ICU and heavily sedated so he doesn't fight the ventilator. We don't know if he has sustained any brain damage from the cardiac arrest, but they shocked him as soon as they saw ventricular fibrillation on the monitor and started giving him arrest medications. I'll take you back now, if you want to see him."

Dr. Stein was nice. He was on call for cardiology that night and if he was annoyed by Max's past, he didn't show it. Just as Dr. Stein had described, Max was heavily sedated to the point of being unconscious. The nurse described it as a "medical coma," so Max's heart and lungs could heal, and he could get the oxygen his body needed without him pulling out his breathing tube. After allowing Donna a few minutes with Max, a nurse escorted her to the ICU waiting room and gave her a blanket and a pillow. She called the family, settled in, and somehow, fell asleep.

The next two days were filled with serial bloodwork, vital signs, x-rays, EKG's, ultrasounds, and a cardiac catheterization. Max's respiratory status had improved to the point of extubation, but instead of being grateful to Donna and everyone else, he was hateful. He had been without alcohol, drugs and nicotine for over a week, and he was not happy about this deprivation. George was the only member of the family to come to the hospital to see Max and be with

Donna. "Well, Max," said Dr. Stein the morning after all the test results had returned, "we have some things to discuss. After we reviewed all the tests you've had over the past couple of days, the team has determined that your heart is no longer able to repair itself. I was surprised when I was called to a cardiac arrest for a 50-year old, but when I reviewed your chart, it answered my questions. Your drug and alcohol use have weakened your heart to the point that it can no longer function properly. We can keep it going mechanically by inserting a left ventricular assist device, or LVAD. The left lower part of your heart is the part that pumps blood out through your body by way of your aorta, the largest artery in the body. Your heart is a muscle, and if that left ventricle is weak, it won't be able to pump enough blood to provide oxygen to your body organs or it may stop pumping altogether and you would have another cardiac arrest. With an LVAD, a mechanical pumping device is surgically implanted in your abdomen and is connected to your left ventricle, from which it pulls blood. The blood is then transported through the mechanical pump system to the aorta, where it distributes blood to the body. The device's battery is contained in a small unit outside of your body that connects to the pump through a wire inserted through the skin. It is portable and does not completely interrupt your life. We will just need to make sure the batteries are always good. We will also implant a defibrillator in your chest. You had a serious episode of ventricular tachycardia followed in the not-too-distant future by sudden death caused by ventricular fibrillation. If you had not been in a hospital when that happened, you would have died. The implanted defibrillator will recognize when your heart has stopped because of ventricular fibrillation and shock it back into a normal rhythm. The heart works two ways. One is by intrinsic electrical activity that moves through the heart and stimulates the muscle to pump blood through your body. The other is the pumping mechanism, which is accomplished by the left ventricle, as I mentioned earlier. Both of yours are defective and these devices will help your heart do its job."

"What's the catch? How long will I have to have these things?" asked Max.

"Well, that might be, in part, up to you," Dr. Stein told him. "In some cases, the LVAD serves to give the heart a chance to rest itself and heal, allowing for its removal, but in most cases it's a bridge to a heart transplant."

"A heart transplant? I'm only 50 years old!" Max said, incredulously.

"I know," said the doctor, "but your lifestyle has aged you beyond those years. Your heart will not serve you much longer. We can insert the LVAD now to prevent another cardiac arrest while we determine the next steps."

Max and Dr. Stein both signed the consent form to have the LVAD implanted and the doctor shook Max's hand and left. Max and Donna sat silently, each with their own thoughts about what was happening to their lives.

"I need a cigarette," Max finally blurted out.

"I don't want to hear it," Donna replied, as authoritatively as she could. "First, there is no smoking in the hospital, and second, smoking is partially to blame for this little visit in the hospital, so don't even mention it again."

She was emboldened by the fact that he was tethered to the bed by tubes and wires and wouldn't be able to reach her even if he wanted to.

"You bitch, you think you're always right," Max managed to retort. "Smoking had nothing to do with this. I don't care what you think. You're the one who stressed me out enough to give me a heart attack."

Donna just let the words slide right down and off her back. By now, she knew all about his narcissistic personality and that he would never change. His words still hurt, but she was getting much better at interpreting them.

The next morning, they wheeled Max up to the operating room for his LVAD implantation and Donna caught a nap while she was waiting. She held off on her morning coffee, hoping to be able to sleep through the procedure, but sleep was restless and before she knew it, he was back.

"The procedure went well. Max will be kept here in ICU again to recover. Tomorrow morning I'll be back to speak with you both about the next steps."

Dr. Stein was a calming presence for Donna. She didn't feel anxious or judged when he spoke with them. After he left, she closed her eyes and tried to rest while Max was still groggy from the sedation that they had given him.

The day was uneventful, except for frequent interruptions for assessments and bloodwork. She enjoyed the time she had to herself while Max was sleeping during the day and then slept in the ICU waiting room at night. She didn't want to chance going to a hotel and not being there if something happened, so she just gratefully accepted the fresh blanket and pillow the nurses always provided for her and tried to sleep as best she could. What she missed most was a good shower and a decent cup of coffee in the morning.

Max awoke the next morning to a round of vital signs and a poke in the arm for blood tests.

"Nurse, don't you ever let anyone rest around here? You just took blood. Why do you need to stick me again? I'm going to need a transfusion if you take any more."

Max was in rare form. Deprived of sleep, alcohol, drugs, and nicotine, he was mean to everyone who came near him. Even the nurses were eager for him to be transferred.

"Good morning, Mr. Miflin. I'm Cindy, a phlebotomist. No one loves to see me coming. I've even been called a vampire, but I just follow the doctor's orders, I don't make them. I'm sorry for the inconvenience."

"Inconvenience? That hurt!" said Max.

"Max, let her alone. She's just doing her job." Donna tried to save the poor girl from any more of Max's verbal poison.

They were saved by Dr. Stein, who came in the room as Cindy left. "Good morning, Max and Donna." Three other people followed.

"These people are members of the transplant team. We want to discuss the process and the requirements for being placed on the transplant list. Hearts are difficult to come by. Many times, the donor has died a traumatic death such as a car accident, severe head injury, or gunshot wound and are determined to be brain dead by extensive neurological testing. As long as the person has a signed organ donor card, his or her organs can be harvested for transplant. If there is no card, the next of kin must give permission, and that can be extremely hard for them. Permission might even be refused. Legally, the next of kin's wishes cannot override those that have been indicated on a signed donor card, but a dispute can delay the process. Understandably, the demand for organs does not meet the supply, and the waiting list is long. For this reason, the requirements for someone to be placed on the transplant list are stringent, and you would have to agree to change your lifestyle completely. No more nicotine, alcohol, or drugs. Any of these things, which are, in large part, responsible for your heart's current failure, would compromise the success of the donor heart and cause it to fail as well. We can't award a heart to someone, even a person as young as you are, if we cannot be assured that they will take care of it. I wanted all these members of the team to be here today as we discuss our decision with you. We have not taken this decision-making process lightly. We struggled with what to do because of your age and otherwise healthy condition, at least at this point. Because of our concerns about your lifestyle, the transplant team from this region has declined your request to be on the transplant list."

Donna's face fell, but Max's just showed arrogance.

"You mean you won't even give me a chance? How do you know I'll start using again? I have been in the hospital without anything for a long time and I'm fine."

"That's because you don't have access to it right now. The hospital is fully in control of what you put in your body. Once you are discharged, all that involuntarily imposed discipline disappears, and you are on your own. With your history of non-compliance, we don't feel that you are a good risk. We may have an option for you, however."

Pointing to a young doctor with a wide smile, Dr. Stein said "This is Dr. Maverick. He has convinced us to contact Duke University Hospital in Durham, North Carolina, and discuss allowing you to be on the transplant list there. Thanks to him, they have agreed, and if you want to do that, we can make it happen. You will have to go there to be evaluated by their team in person and solemnly agree to refrain from all the things we discussed. You will be monitored closely for compliance and if you mess up even once, you will be off the transplant list. You will need to move to the Durham area because this will be a lifetime commitment. The other option is to live with your LVAD for the rest of your life, which will be greatly shortened compared to your life with a new heart. You can discuss it with your wife and let us know tomorrow morning."

# Chapter 16

Have a Heart

Max needed a heart transplant to live. Donna and Max absorbed this reality slowly, one scene at a time. They had lived in New Jersey all their lives, and now they faced the possibility they would have to pick up and transplant themselves, too, but they wanted to give Max a shot at living. Donna tried to look at the situation from a positive stance. Maybe this is what they needed. They would be moving away from all the friends and negative influences that Max had in his life. Maybe they really could start over. New home, new heart, new social circle. For the first time in a long time, Donna could see some hope in a seemingly hopeless situation. It would be good for everyone. They decided together that this was the right move for them. They went through all the red tape that was required of potential organ recipients at Duke University Hospital and put their home in New Jersey on the market. Max was sternly warned that there would be no second chances. Only one strike and he was out. He had to stay clean.

They sold their home and found a beautiful new Victorian home in Wake Forest, North Carolina, a lovely community that was away from the busy streets and neighborhoods of Durham but close enough to Duke that Max could get there quickly if a call would come in that a donor was available. It was the prettiest house in the neighborhood. Donna enrolled Alex in school, set up the house, located the shopping areas, and waited for the bittersweet phone call from the transplant team that a donor was available. She knew what that meant: that another family, somewhere, had just lost a loved one to tragedy, and she prayed that Max would appreciate their sacrifice and protect the gift he would be receiving.

Max had to join Alcoholics Anonymous (AA) as part of his agreement with the Duke doctors, and he had to establish care with a psychiatrist. Weekly meetings didn't come close to providing Max with the care and support he needed to break free from such a sticky web of addiction. A stubborn deterrent to effective therapy was that Max still could not accept responsibility for anything going wrong in his life, and he continued to blame Donna for everything, even in therapy, negating any positive impact on his mental state that may have been achieved.

Max knew his actions were wrong, but he couldn't admit responsibility for the cause of the effect. He knew his anger was fueled by substance abuse, but like most addicts, he found it difficult to change since he could never admit that he was the cause of his own anger and frustrations.

"I'm Max, and I am an addict. I'm addicted to alcohol and drugs, and I'm here because I'm on the heart transplant list, and it's a requirement."

"Hello, Max," came the collective reply from the room.

The leader let Max's qualifying statement pass, for the time being. There would be time enough for exploration into those feelings later. One by one, the members of the group introduced themselves. Max looked around and felt he didn't belong there with these people. He was better than them, but he felt he had to stay. They said a prayer and did a reading from the *Big Book*, the basic textbook of Alcoholics Anonymous.

The *Big Book* is one of the best-selling books of all time, which is a sober testament to the gravity of the alcoholism problem. Many AA groups also allow those addicted to other substances or behaviors as well as alcohol. Its renowned Twelve Step Program has helped innumerable people achieve and maintain sobriety since 1936, but it is not an easy process, and not everyone makes it. One basic tenet of the program is a belief in a higher power and the faith that you are not alone. Prayer is a large part of recovery from addiction and one in which Max freely took part. He wasn't what one would call an active, practicing Christian, but he did believe in God, and had no problem talking to Him within the confines of the walls at the AA meetings. Outside that, he never discussed his faith much, at least not with Donna.

AA participants are also required to keep a journal to record notes from meetings, write down thoughts and feelings, and experience catharsis. Having access to Max's AA journal has provided me with insight into who he was. His sober self was unlike his impaired self in many ways. Max was like a Harlequin mask: smiling one minute, crying the next, or maybe it was anger. He appeared to be a tortured soul inside, knowing what he had to do but powerless to defeat the forces causing his torment. I want to believe that is true for many abusers. I would like to think that they don't want to be who they are but lack the fortitude to resist their violent urges. They are people, too, and, just as you and I, are a combination of good and bad. Without wishing to be repetitive, I will call up the memory of Donna's account of Max's childhood from earlier in the book as a prerequisite to my next words: affluent, alcoholic and absentee parents, being left alone to his own devices, tossed out like an old dishrag as a teenager by his mother when his father left her for his secretary, etc. Common among abusers, Max had a narcissistic personality. Some of the hallmarks of narcissism are lack of empathy, a need for admiration, arrogance, self-centeredness, manipulation, and being demanding of others, while refusing to take responsibility for anything themselves.[18] Although the exact cause of these traits is not well-understood, it is felt that a combination of nature and nurture, as we have already seen is true for so many aspects of our beings, mix it up to form these traits. Unfortunately, the actual personality disorder of narcissism is difficult to treat because these people don't think there is anything wrong with them; they feel everything bad that happens is someone else's fault, not their own. It's a well-accepted tenet that you can't help someone who doesn't feel they need help, and that pretty much describes a narcissist. Although she was able to see the good in Max, Donna's accounts of him spelled narcissism, and her accounts of life with him are largely disturbing. They are also backed up by Max, himself. In his journal, he admits to treating his family poorly, to possessing all these characteristics, either directly or indirectly, and he even uses the word narcissistic to describe himself at one point. When he was sober, he had an incredible self-awareness of who he wanted to be, and, in turn, of the person he turned into while he was impaired, like a Dr. Jekyll and a Mr. Hyde, albeit a bit less loathsome.

Not unlike the outwardly haughty Cowardly Lion from the Wizard of Oz, beneath the layer of anger in Max was an insecure, terrified soul, who didn't really believe that he had the courage to overcome his adversarial self. He picked on people weaker than he was to appear fierce and to prove himself a force with which to be reckoned. Unlike the fabled lion, however, it took more than a slap across the face to make Max see the error of his ways. It took him staring into the face of death to get him to an AA meeting, which then required him to peel all the layers of the onion off until he got to the core of who he was, and he did. He even wrote a letter to Gina apologizing for how he had treated her and their family and thanking her for everything she had done for them. It was a heartfelt and almost tear-jerking letter, but even here, he strayed back to a "not all my fault" theme at times. Donna made a point of telling me that he never wrote a letter to her like that. Sadly, once outside the secure, comfortable walls of the AA meetings, he found it impossible to hold onto the strength that had been generated within those walls, and whatever protective mechanisms he had honed at the meetings collapsed in the face of life in the real world.

Max was also a consummate liar, such a convincing one that even his brother, sister, and mother supported his accusations that Donna was to blame for his failing emotional health and descent into addiction, even though that journey had started long before they met. Considering his mother, that makes sense, since she could never take responsibility for her own shortcomings either, as was previously noted. She wasn't going to blame herself for Max's problems. She and Donna got along in the beginning, until Donna started bringing Max's problems to the family's attention, and then she became an instant nemesis in their lives. Others in the family suffered from addiction as well, so no one wanted to look at Max because if they did, they would have had to look in their mirrors and see themselves.

There is a proven genetic connection to addiction, be it nicotine, alcohol, or drugs. In fact, studies have shown that even up to half of a person's risk for addiction can be attributed to his or her genetic make-up.[19] Tangible as genetic sequencing may be, it is essential to consider environment as a factor in the disease of addiction, just as we did with criminal behavior and poor decision-making. Environmental factors can be controlled by how you react to them, unlike your inherited DNA. These influences have been proven to affect the way certain gene markers are expressed.[20] For instance, identical twins have identical genetic make-up and most of the markers that define things such as physical features will remain prominent in both, but environmental circumstances can serve as influencers as to how a person's character or personality unfolds. Living conditions, degree of family support, education, availability of economic and other resources, and the influences of other people in one's life are some of the things that can affect genetic make-up so that even identical twins can exhibit different characteristics when raised in different environments. In addition, it is believed that these influencers can even change the genetic makeup of a person to the extent that the altered gene can be passed on to future generations, which may explain similarities in familial traits and habits, such as abusive behavior.[21] Although eerily similar stories of twins who were separated at birth, both good and evil, have been published, environmental influences could also lend credence to the evil twin story lines that the cinema loves. Perhaps that scientific finding was a major contributor to Max's adult characteristics. Listening to Max's accounts as told to Donna, the question of his own mother's mental health must be entered into the equation of additive factors that contributed to his demise. Maybe narcissistic behavior started with her or maybe it started with relatives in past generations and the cycle just could not be broken. By looking at all of these biological and external events that can team up to cause unhappiness, it's clear that although we have no control over some of them, we can make conscious choices to start in motion new, positive influences that can disrupt destructive cycles, and we must, for these cycles of abuse to end.

Once you dissect the details of an abuser's world, past and present, an image can begin to appear that may tend to explain his despicable behavior. We can understand, and maybe even pity, someone whose own personal black hole is visible enough to explain away the destructive actions that are negatively impacting someone else's life. However, we can never excuse violating the rights of others; this behavior is never, ever, acceptable. Understanding is fine and good, but never acceptance. Nothing short of self-defense should give anyone legitimate cause to intentionally hurt another person or treat them with disrespect. Conversely, no one should allow themselves to be convinced that they bring it on themselves, or that it is somehow their fault that the abuser is the way he or she is. Max tried that with Donna, and even if she didn't really believe it deep inside, it was enough to knock her self-esteem down a few notches with each insult. Note to victims: The cycle of abuse must stop, and it can stop with you. I won't lie and tell you it's easy, but it's worth giving it everything you have in order to win your freedom and your peace, because you deserve it. There will be suggestions on how to help yourself later in the book. There are plenty of success stories. You can be the next one.

# Chapter 17

Nicotine Wins a Battle

The ride into Durham, North Carolina from their home was not a long drive but the tension in the car made it feel like hours. Moving is considered a significant life stressor, but when you add the problems Donna and Max were experiencing, it increased the stress in their lives exponentially. Donna suspected Max was still using, and the little angel he gave her from AA as proof of his sobriety was more like proof of his lies. She knew coins that looked like poker chips were the rewards for sobriety, not little angels. Oh, he may have gotten it from someone in his class, his mentor, or the group's leader, as a reminder that his guardian angel is with him, but not as a measure of sobriety. And he was particularly irritable today because he knew they would be checking his blood and urine for evidence of chemical substances and so he was unable to get himself a fix. If he was found to be using, again, he would be off the transplant list.

"This fucking traffic is as bad here as it was in New Jersey," Max complained as he laid a heavy hand on the horn and gestured menacingly at the driver who tried to pull in front of him. Donna knew he shouldn't be driving anymore, but he was not about to give up one of the last bastions of control he had over his life, and she was too tired to fight with him about it.

"Settle down," Donna said. "It's bad, but you won't change anything by getting upset. You'll only hurt yourself."

"Shut up, you stupid broad," he mumbled under his breath.

She chose not to pursue the issue.

"There's the parking lot," she said. "Just pull in and let's get to the office so you're not late."

"This place is a mess. I think they try to make it as confusing as they can for people. Look how far we have to walk to get to the Cardiology office. I think it will kill me just getting there."

Indeed, the Duke University Medical Center is a massive enterprise and is a part of the Duke University Health System, a world-renowned educational, medical, and research maze of buildings that includes Duke University, home to the School of Medicine and the School of Nursing, among others; the inpatient hospital; numerous diagnostic, medical and surgical offices and suites; a large Children's Hospital; and many off-campus facilities providing similar services. It currently encompasses over 200 acres of property and about 7.5 million square feet of office space. There was a very good reason why Max's doctors in New Jersey sent him to Duke.

"Max, all we have to do is walk from the parking garage to the building and then one of the volunteers can push you to the cardiology office in a wheelchair. It isn't that bad."

"No. No one is pushing me in a wheelchair. I'm fine," Max retorted.

"Suit yourself," Donna said, but she stayed close by his side as they slowly made their way through the wide, bright, impressive corridors of Duke to the heart specialists' office.

Max was visibly short of breath when he arrived, but he discounted its importance. Always denial.

"Max Miflin?" the nurse called.

"Yes, I'm coming." He tried to hide his trouble breathing but that's something that's hard to get past a trained cardiology nurse. He allowed Donna to accompany him into the exam room, for which she was grateful. She never knew if he would tell her everything the doctor said.

"Are you okay, Mr. Miflin? Where is your oxygen tank?"

"I don't need it. I just walked further than I usually do. I'll be fine."

The nurse seated Max in a room, took his vital signs and prepared him for the doctor, helping him into a gown, checking his LVAD and implanted defibrillator, asking lots of questions, drawing his blood, and weighing him. Lastly, she gave him the little plastic cup and directed him to the bathroom. She noted that his oxygen level was a little lower than she would have liked but he seemed to be breathing better and she decided to recheck it before he left, after he had rested.

"Hello, Mr. Miflin. I'm Dr. Martin. How are you today?"

Resident doctors always saw Duke patients first because it's a teaching facility, then the real doctors, as Max called them, came in. He thought the residents always looked young.

"I'm okay. I just want to get this over with and go home."

Dr. Martin looked at Max's chart, not addressing his obvious impatience with the visit.

"It looks like your oxygen level is a little low. It seems you didn't bring your tank with you today. You will probably need to wear it a little more often than you do now. Until a donor heart becomes available, yours will probably continue to weaken, so you will have to use the supplemental oxygen to make sure your body gets what it needs."

Max nodded understanding and answered yes to all the other questions. Are you taking your medications? Are you trying to be as active as possible? Is your appetite good? Are you watching your salt intake? Is your pain under control? Are you going to your AA meetings? Are you staying sober? Are you still avoiding nicotine? He fibbed a little on that last one. He couldn't give up everything so Max figured a few cigarettes now and then wouldn't hurt, and how would they know, anyway? He'd made sure he had clean-smelling clothes on and didn't have any cigarettes before the visit. Donna knew better but didn't dare intervene. Max was glad when the resident left and Dr. Gambino, his "real" doctor, came in.

"Hi, Max. It looks like you are staying stable for now."

Dr. Gambino was the best cardiologist around but lacked bedside manner. Max didn't care; he wasn't interested in small talk. He just wanted to be cleared and go home.

"Pending the results of your blood tests, it seems we can keep you on the transplant list. You know donor hearts are hard to come by, so it's going to be very important for you to take care of yourself and behave. If you go off the straight-and-narrow someone else will take your place."

"I know," Max said.

"Good. Well, keep up the good work and keep that oxygen tank with you from now on. I'll have the nurse recheck your oxygen level. If it's acceptable, then you can go. Don't forget to make your next appointment on the way out."

Dr. Gambino shook his hand and left the room. The nurse came in a few minutes later and put the oximeter on his finger. It took a little while to register because his heart condition affected his circulation and the oxygen level wasn't registering. The nurse gave him a small warm pack for his hand to stimulate the flow of blood to his fingertip. The little light sensor in the oximeter had to pick up the oxygen in the blood reaching his fingertips, an end point of circulation, to get an accurate assessment of whether or not the rest of the organs in his body were receiving their fair share. The warmth helped, and finally, an acceptable result displayed on the device. Donna checked Max out and slipped her arm beneath his, trying to avoid the appearance of supporting him as he walked. It took a while to reach the car and Donna let him stop and catch his breath before they began the trek back home to Wake Forest to await the phone call that would save Max's life.

"I'm going to stay outside for some fresh air," said Max as they arrived home.

Donna nodded but knew it wasn't fresh air he was after. He hadn't had a cigarette since the day before, and although he never admitted it to her, she could smell cigarette smoke from a mile away.

"You know, Max, if you are going to smoke, you can't do it while your oxygen is on because it can explode," Donna reminded him.

"It's none of your business if I smoke or not," Max admonished her. "And how many times have you ever read about a patient being blown up while smoking around oxygen? You can't tell on me because then it will be your fault if I don't get a new heart and I die."

Donna knew that this was, in the short term, true. She certainly wasn't responsible for the chronic heart disease plaguing Max, but if he was taken off the transplant list because she ratted him out to the doctor about his smoking, she would, ultimately, be responsible for his death in her mind. She sighed and just let him be, with a mental note to herself to stay far away if he was smoking with the oxygen running. She didn't have to mull this over too long, though, just until the next morning when they received a phone call from the hospital.

"Hello, is this Donna Miflin?" a male voice asked.

"Yes," Donna replied.

"This is Dr. Gambino. I'm afraid I have some bad news. We got Max's bloodwork back and it showed high levels of nicotine in his blood. We cannot keep him on the heart transplant list any longer. I understand that the doctors in New Jersey wouldn't approve him because of his substance abuse, but one of them convinced us to give him a shot because of his age. We did that, but he failed to hold up his end and we can't sacrifice a donor heart for someone who will not be compliant with his care."

"Oh, no," Donna said. "That's terrible news. I didn't even know you could test for nicotine in the blood. He would never admit to me he was smoking again, but I guess this is the proof."

"Yes, nicotine can stay in the blood for up to 3 days. We didn't notice any tobacco odor at his visit but that's why we include this particular test, to make sure patients haven't only given it up for one day. Nicotine is very bad for the heart. I'm sorry it turned out this way for him. Tell him he needs to keep the appointment he made because we still have to monitor his LVAD and defibrillator."

Donna thanked him and hung up the phone. Anger, fear and resentment overtook her, and the adrenaline surge pushed her over the edge.

"That was Dr. Gambino! Do you know what you have done?" Donna screamed. "You just couldn't give up those cigarettes, could you?! You will never get a heart now! They have taken you off the heart transplant list!"

"What did you do!? Did you squeal?" Max yelled back. "Did you think this was an easy way to kill me? Well, now it WILL be your fault! You should have stayed in Auschwitz, you skinny bitch!"

That was just one of Max's denigrating terms for Donna because of her slight frame. It usually cut her deeply, but today she just let it roll off her back.

"No, you jerk!" she yelled again. "They found nicotine in your blood. How did you think you were going to get away with that?"

"You're lying. I never heard of them testing for nicotine. I'll bet you just couldn't wait to spill the beans, could you!"

"You ass! No, I didn't spill the beans, and I didn't know there was a test for that, either. Dr. Gambino said nicotine can stay in your system for up to three days. You thought you were so smart not smoking for a day before your appointment."

Donna's emotions were spent. She didn't know how much more she could take. There were some days she wished Max would have been successful in poisoning her the time she thinks he may have tried. If he really was putting something poisonous into her drinks or food, she doesn't know why he stopped—a moment of conscience, she guessed, or maybe her doctor's suspicions struck fear into him. In any case, it didn't work, she couldn't prove he had even tried, and here she was now, faced with Max's almost certain death without the benefit of a new heart. She heard the door slam, the car engine start, and the squeal of tires on the driveway. She heard the loud blare of a horn and a second set of squealing tires as another driver slammed on the brakes. No crash, two engines starting up and the sound of two cars driving away. She couldn't even muster up enough emotion to worry.

# Chapter 18

Demons for the Win

Despite Donna's continued efforts to help Max, his physical and emotional condition deteriorated, and his drug abuse persisted. He was losing control and he knew it. His behavior had been bad enough when he was still able to maintain some control in his life, but now his world was crumbling, and the loss of control for someone like him was unbearable.

It was abundantly clear that Max was also in serious financial straits. Before they left New Jersey, he had taken out a business loan for $400,000, with their home as collateral, and without Donna's knowledge. Someone had signed the papers in her name. She wasn't sure whether he forged her name or someone else stood in for her as the documents were signed, but she did know that she was not the one approving that transaction. She wondered where he had gotten the money when she refused to sign for him in the car that day.

Previously, he had taken the check Donna had been given from her stepfather's will and cashed it himself, telling her that because they were married, the money was his, too. When they sold their house in New Jersey, he refused to give her any money from the sale, and she had to resort to stealing checks from him and signing his name to get money for grocery shopping. What saved Donna, financially, is that they had put their new home in Wake Forest under her name so the bank couldn't come after that to pay for the business loan. Max had a partner in his business, and he was supposed to have been handling the details and making the monthly payments, which he was not doing, making the bank quite unhappy. Donna was receiving multiple threatening collections calls, and it took lawyers in three states to finally end the financial fiasco.

In addition to his monetary asset decline, Max's health continued to worsen. He was becoming weaker, and without the possibility of a new heart, he knew his time in this life was limited. The almost complete loss of control made Max more abusive than ever and his anger was spiraling upward. As his rage increased, Donna's tolerance was spiraling downward. His verbal abuse was escalating, He was spitting at her and throwing things at her. He was even writing abusive emails to himself, signing her name and then copying his brother, Danny, on them. Finally, in desperation, she took out a protection from abuse order. He wasn't weak enough, yet, that infirmity would offer her any protection from him, and being frail herself, she decided she could not take that chance.

A deputy sheriff came to the house so Max could collect his belongings and be escorted out in accordance with the protection from abuse order, but he continued his loud verbal abuse while in the presence of law enforcement. Even in this state, however, Max still managed to appear the pathetic one, and Donna could sense sympathy from the deputy sheriff as they hauled him away. They knew he was sick, and again, Donna seemed like the bad one. She did feel guilty but deemed that hers and her son's safety trumped Max's needs at this point.

"Donna! Where are you!"

Donna froze at the unexpected sound of his Max's voice several days later. How did he get in? Did she or Alex go out and forget to lock the door when they came back in? She ran to the foyer, where Max was obviously high and or drunk, pacing around and yelling. Highly agitated, he went from room to room, and as he exited the rooms, Donna locked the doors behind him, which only served to fuel the fire that was raging in his heart.

"Max, you have to leave. You know you can't be here."

"It's my house, too! You can't kick me out! I have a right to be here!" he screamed.

Frightened, Alex stood by, watching it all unfold.

"Alex, go down the street to the neighbor's house," she directed as she dialed the Sheriff's office. "I'll let you know when you can come back."

Alex did as he was told, and Donna continued to try and calm Max down. He did leave the house, but not the premises. She watched him run to the shed, retrieve a pair of garden shears and rush back towards the house, yelling, "If I'm going to die, I'm taking you with me!"

She felt the color drain from her face, her skin clammy, and her heart pounding. She doublechecked that all the doors were locked and then returned to a vantage point where she could safely watch his movements. Thankfully, before he could reach the house, the Sheriff's Deputies arrived, sirens wailing. They surrounded Max, trying to talk him into dropping the shears, which he finally did, but not before cutting the cord to the LVAD that was keeping him alive. Horrified, Donna called 911 and soon the sound of sirens filled the air again as an ambulance sped up the road to their house. Miraculously, Max survived the interruption to his life-supporting device, and he was rushed to Duke Hospital, where they repaired the LVAD. The doctors told Donna that, ironically, the adrenaline produced from his drug use probably had sustained his heart until they could repair the LVAD. Max was like a cat with everyone wondering when it would be time for that ninth life to be over.

Now there was no choice. Donna had to take him back; he needed a caregiver. It was getting harder for him to get access to drugs as his activity level waned, but he continued to smoke cigarettes and drink, and at this point, what would be the advantage to making him stop? She tried, but it wasn't worth the hassle when they both knew stopping wasn't going to help him. His habits might hasten his death, but if he enjoyed them in the remaining days he had left, there was little cause to make him stop. The doctor told

Donna that Max should still try to remain as active as he could but suggested that she contact a hospice service because Max probably only had a few months left to his life.

Hospices services are available to terminally ill patients whose doctors have agreed that they will only have six months or less to live if the disease runs its expected course. Hospice companies provide a Registered Nurse to come to patients' homes once a week, or more, if needed, to assess their condition, make sure they have all of the medicines they need, keep pain under as much control as possible, and provide support to families. The nurses are then in touch with the doctor for any needs or changes in the condition of the patient. Hospice can also provide home health aides to help with a patient's activities of daily living, sometimes with light housework, and they have chaplains on staff if spiritual care is requested. They have social workers who can help navigate family matters, living situations, etc. These services allow for gravely ill patients to spend their last days in the comfort of their own homes with their loved ones. There are no heroic measures involved; it's strictly palliative, or comfort, care. Unless a patient or family requests it, there are no hospitalizations; all treatments are accomplished in the home. Donna and Max signed on for the hospice services and the next day, his nurse came for her first visit.

"Hello, Mrs. Miflin. I'm Anne from Hospice Services here to check on Mr. Miflin."

"Hi, Anne. Call me Donna. I'll take you to Max."

Donna escorted Anne into the living room where Max was sitting on a chair.

"Hi, Mr. Miflin. I'm Anne and I'll be seeing you once a week to check on you and see if you need anything. How have you been feeling?"

"Okay. What do you need to do?" Max asked, curtly.

"Well, each time I come I'll be checking your vital signs, making sure you aren't having any pain, check your medicines, and see if you need any help with anything. We have a social worker who can help you with any financial issues regarding hospice services or any problems in the home. We also have a chaplain on our team, and he will come out any time you feel the need for spiritual services. I'm not supposed to do this, but I'm going to give Donna my cell phone number. I'm the only hospice nurse in this Home Health company and no one else knows much about hospice care, so I take calls for my own patients unless I am away. I live in Cary, so it may take me a while to get here, but Donna can call me any time she wants with any questions. If I can help you over the phone, I will, and if I can't, I'll come out."

"Thank you," said Donna, and Max acknowledged Anne's information with a nod.

After two years in hospice nursing, Anne still was having a hard time fighting her ingrained emergency nursing instincts to check and treat patients with an eye to improvement or cure instead of palliative care.

"This thing is keeping me alive," Max said, pointing to the external power device connected to his LVAD. "And this jump starts my heart if it stops beating," Max said as he showed Anne where the defibrillator was implanted.

Ann nodded. "Yes, I read your chart and I'm familiar with your case and with your devices," Anne assured him. She checked his blood pressure, which was hard to hear and on the low side, and felt his pulse, which was weak but there. His breathing was stable, but he was connected to an oxygen tank to help feed his body organs with the oxygen that his heart could no longer supply very well.

"I get tired easily, but I can still get around the house, and I don't have a lot of pain. I'm not very hungry most of the time."

"But you have to eat," interjected Donna, who had been quiet up until now.

Max gave her a look that made Anne feel sorry for Donna. It was an unsettling look, one that needed no words to explain what he was thinking. He turned back to look at Anne and continued their conversation about his health needs.

"It looks like you have enough of all of your regular medications. I'm going to order a prescription drug called Roxanol for you, in case you have pain or difficulty breathing. It is a very concentrated, liquid form of morphine. Obviously, it can help with pain, but it can also help when breathing becomes difficult by relaxing the blood vessels in the lungs and slowing your respirations. It can also help with anxiety. Roxanol can be given every four hours in very small doses measured in drops to put under your tongue. This is because if you begin to have trouble swallowing or become unconscious, the medicine can be put under your tongue and it will be absorbed into your system that way. We'll start out with a low dose, but we can gradually increase it, to a certain point, based on your pain level and degree of difficulty breathing. Too much, though, can slow respirations to a dangerous level. It's an opioid, and that's what opioids can do."

Donna shot Max a concerned look, which Anne could tell that his peripheral vision caught, but which he ignored. Anne sensed an anxiety in Donna that she wasn't sure was due to Max's illness or something else.

"I'm here to keep you comfortable. You will begin to notice changes in your body as the time gets closer. I'll give you a pamphlet on what to expect at the end of life. I would like you two to read it over and I will answer any questions you have at my next visit. As these changes occur, I'll do what I can to make it easier for you."

Max sat stone-faced through the whole visit, responding only when he needed to. Anne scheduled an appointment with them for her next visit, said goodbye, and Donna walked Anne to the door.

"Are you okay, Donna?" Anne asked. She seemed a bit jumpy and nervous to her.

"Yes, I'm fine," Donna answered unconvincingly. "This is just a lot to deal with."

"I know, this is hard on everyone. I want you to keep the Roxanol out of his reach, so he doesn't dose himself." Anne gave Donna a knowing look and Donna nodded her understanding.

"Please don't hesitate to call me if you need anything at all. Max is the patient, but family members matter almost as much, if not more, sometimes."

"I will," said Donna, truthfully.

Anne could tell that Donna was appreciative, but she left with an uneasy feeling that she wasn't getting the whole story.

The next visit showed Max feeling weaker. He was still getting around but not quite as much. Anne immediately noticed the cigarette burning in the ashtray near his oxygen tank and the glass that contained something that did not look like water or juice. She also saw a handsome young man with wavy dark hair in soccer clothes come into the house.

"Anne, this is our son, Alex," said Donna.

"Hi, Alex. It's nice to meet you."

In pure adolescent discomfort, Alex said hello and immediately disappeared up the stairs.

"What a handsome son you have," Anne told Max and Donna.

Donna thanked her and Max nodded his head.

"Does your doctor know you are still smoking, Max?" Anne asked.

"What difference does it make? I'm dying."

"I understand that, and it does make some sense, but it's dangerous to smoke while oxygen is in use, and it may make your breathing even harder than it is getting."

The way Max looked at her gave Anne the shivers. It had the same undertones that were in the look he gave Donna when she interjected her feeling about his eating at the last visit.

"Duly noted," he replied.

Anne finished the visit and Donna again walked her to the door.

"Donna, I'm worried about you. You seem nervous, and I feel like there is something you are not saying. Please let me help."

Donna looked at Anne like she might have wanted to say something but couldn't. She kept glancing back toward the living room where Max was seated.

"No, I'm really okay. I don't need anything."

"Well, we have a social worker and a chaplain that would gladly come out and visit with you or Max, or both. And you know you can call me at any time, too."

"I know," said Donna.

All the way home, Anne thought about Max and Donna. She thought about the impatient way he spoke to her and how she jumped to get him what he wanted. Something was not right, but she couldn't force Donna to share or get her any help if she didn't want it. The only thing that put Anne's mind at ease was the knowledge that Max was growing weaker, and if there was something gravely wrong there, he would be too weak to hurt her. There would only be one or two more visits for Anne to the Miflin home.

Donna felt chills running up and down her spine as Max had her drive him to Duke one morning because he wanted his defibrillator turned off. She knew he was giving up, and she couldn't blame him. Turning the defibrillator off would not hasten his death but it would prevent his life from being saved if his heart went into the lethal ventricular fibrillation dysrhythmia. She also suspected that he had stopped taking his medicine. His mood was mellow that day and he told Donna how sorry he was about how he had treated her, and that he never knew what he had with her until now. He thanked her for everything she had done for him and told her he loved her. Once home from Duke, sans defibrillator, he asked to speak with his brother, and Donna dialed his number. She was grateful that Danny was available to speak with Max, then she got on the phone and asked Danny if he would be able to come by the next day to see Max, to which he agreed. The trip from New Jersey to North Carolina was long, so Danny left as soon as he could. Max wanted to see his mom, too, but when Donna called and explained the situation to her, Irene said she couldn't make the trip from Virginia because her two chihuahuas were not doing well and she couldn't leave them. She said she would call him the next day. Donna thought how fitting her lack of concern for her son was, even in his last days.

Danny did make it to see Max the next day and he was glad he did, but their mother did not, just as she had said.

"Please put that drink down, and no cigarettes. Did you not hear what the doctor said?" Donna reprimanded Max.

She knew the fight was over so she couldn't see what good would come out of depriving him of the things he loved so she had been trying to go easy on him, but today, he seemed different. His color looked pale and his breathing seemed to be a little more strained. In stark contrast to yesterday's proclamation of love and apologies, Max suddenly became Max once again.

"Shut up, you stupid cunt. I'll do what I want. You only hear what you want to hear. If you think I'm going to leave you anything, you're fucking crazy. I'm healthier than you, you sick bitch."

Donna ignored the hurtful comments and sat down by his bed while he fell asleep. He had been getting fatigued more easily and was sleeping more than before, both things about which she had read in the end of life brochure. She dozed off, too, but was awakened by a sudden raspy sound, and she watched as Max struggled to breathe, his respirations rattling with each slow, agonized breath. She grabbed the phone and called Anne.

"Please hurry, Anne! I think I'm losing him!" she cried into the phone.

"Okay, I'll be there as soon as I can," Anne said.

Donna jumped up on the bed with him, oblivious to the cigarette smoldering near the running oxygen tank. This was it, and she wasn't ready. She grabbed his arm.

"Please, Max, no! Please don't leave me! I need you!" she sobbed.

As she saw the cigarette burning down to ashes and looked at the half of a glass of cognac that was sitting on the bedside stand, she was reminded of the devastation they caused for Max, for her, and for their family. Rapid, painful memories flooded in and she could see what her life with him had really been like. She remembered when she went into early labor at six months with Alex. Even the nurses knew Max was high. Naturally, one doesn't expect to be going to the hospital to deliver a six-month gestation baby, so Max couldn't prepare and choose sobriety for the event. However, Donna's was a high-risk pregnancy because of her Lupus, so readiness should have been an ongoing state for him. He had no excuse, however, a few months prior to this present day when Alex had to have a kidney biopsy done. It was a scheduled procedure, so Max knew where to go and when he had to be there, but he still showed up high.

Reality was dawning, and as these incidences filled her head, he took his last breath, and she let go of him, finally, and permanently. She stopped crying and covered him with the sheet that he always kicked off. Robotically she turned off the oxygen tank, took the mask off his face, snuffed out his last cigarette, and gently pushed his eyes closed. She tossed the cognac down the sink and sat down on the chair by the bed to wait for Anne to come and pronounce him dead. Since Cary, North Carolina was quite a drive from Wake Forest, and based on Donna's very anxious call, Anne knew she wouldn't make it in time. She stayed with Donna until after the funeral director arrived to take Max away.

In her solitude, Donna pondered why she had stayed with him as long as she had, and what she might have done had he not become sick and died. She had been terrified of him. Terrified of how worthless he had made her feel; terrified of his strength, his power, and his substance-fueled rage; terrified of being alone; terrified of the destitution that would have accompanied a loss of income; terrified of being a single mother; terrified of how she would help her own aging mother if she would leave the house; terrified of losing her child; and terrified of being sick with no one to take care of her. She was terrified to leave him. Adding to this all-encompassing fear was a lingering guilt about not seeing her father before he died. He had wanted her to come and see him in the hospital after he had a stroke and she refused, punishing him for not being the father she had wanted and deserved. That emotional decision had been like an albatross around Donna's neck ever since then, and she swore, when Max got sick, that she would not do the same to him, no matter how much he hurt her. She wanted no more albatrosses holding her life hostage. She reminded herself that Max had caused his own death.

Donna was not responsible for Max's happiness and well-being. She should not have felt that her sense of self was predicated on Max's happiness. If you find yourself falling victim to this mindset, or if you feel that you are responsible for helping someone who is abusing you, it's time to switch gears. You did not make your abuser the person that he is, and you are not responsible for his getting treatment for whatever character flaws he has that are complicating his life. I would never say not to guide him toward the help he needs, but that is where your responsibility ends. Help him as you are able, while at the same time protecting yourself. People must help themselves, and be serious about recovery, if they are ever to become independently functioning people.

While you are guiding him to help, why not think about why you accept this behavior from him, especially if you have had more than one experience with an abusive partner? Repetitive patterns of being drawn to these kinds of men may spell issues for you that could be contributing to the choices you make. You may be a co-dependent person, someone who derives some sort of satisfaction from a toxic relationship, such as fulfilling a need to be needed by allowing the bad behavior of a loved one to continue. Even if this is not true, seek out a professional counselor, anyway. He or she can help you sort out your own emotions and the behaviors that result from them or help you deal with the issues at hand, namely your current abuse. A counselor is an integral part of the healing process. It is not a sign of weakness to seek help; it is a sign of strength. We all have issues, and probably more people than not should be seeking help but don't because they are embarrassed. It's nothing to be ashamed of. Be strong and be healthy.

# Chapter 19

Finally, at Peace

Max's son, Carl, had been planning his wedding for Oct 6, 2007, and it was to be at the elegant, stately Miflin house on a dock overlooking their beautiful private lake. When Max's condition began deteriorating, this date, unfortunately, would coincide with that of his life expectancy. Max wanted Carl to postpone the wedding because it might be too hard on everyone. Carl, however, refused to change the couple's plans, instead stating that he had dealt with enough already, and the wedding date would stand. Normally, a wedding is a difficult event to postpone, but given that it was being held at a private residence, there would be no need to cancel a church for the ceremony or a sought-after venue for the reception, so a change could have been made without a terrible degree of difficulty. Carl was as tired as anyone else of the upheavals in his life.

As it turned out, Max died on September 23, 2007, and the beat went on. A beautiful, joyous wedding was held as planned and everyone irreverently partied as though nothing had happened. There was no mourning then or even at the funeral, which was held the next day. Max was cremated and his ashes placed in an urn, as is customary. He had chosen the funeral home and planned his service, which must be a surreal experience for anyone. He had chosen the "February Song" by Josh Grobin; and "I Know You Are Out There Somewhere" by the Moody Blues, for the music to be played. He chose the poem "The Dash," by Linda Ellis for recitation. Each of these selections is profoundly introspective of life from a retrospective and often melancholy aspect. Donna didn't know what Max was trying to say by choosing these words for his final message. Maybe he was making a sincere apology that could no longer be followed by insults. Or maybe it was regret for things done and things left undone. Donna thought he was expressing sadness for things that could have been. I suspect it might have been all the above. She wanted to believe that he would have been different if he had only made different choices.

Even those touching words, though, couldn't move the would-be mourners. No one cried. No one sent memorials to the Heart Association fund that Donna had set up in his name and had announced in his obituary. His mother and one of his sisters didn't even make an appearance at the funeral or the wedding. They were protesting because the wedding had not been postponed and people were disrespecting Max by celebrating right after his death, or so the mom said. She said she wouldn't go to the funeral because she believed it was all Donna's fault that Max was dead, and she even faked an illness, herself, so her daughter would have to stay home to take care of her. Of course, she didn't attend Max's brother, Danny's wedding, either because "the cunt" (their father's wife and his reason for leaving her) would be there. Max and Danny's father and his wife were there for Max's funeral and Carl's wedding, too, so you know the real reason Irene missed both her grandson's wedding and her son's funeral.

Knowing about his mother's actions for the most important days of her sons' lives and for the event of Max's death, consider what kind of role model Max had as his guide throughout his early years. You will see a considerable dearth of nurturing that explains, at least in part, Max's myriad of problems. Nurture over nature.

Donna almost broke down once at the funeral but was immediately grabbed by their son, Alex, who said "Don't you dare cry. He doesn't deserve it." Alex has never cried that Donna knows of since Max had been cremated, and Donna picked out a nice urn to hold his ashes. She noticed that the urn in the service was not the same one she had chosen and thought it odd. After the service she approached the funeral director and asked why it had been changed.

"Don't worry, Donna," the Director told her. "Max's ashes are being kept safely in the urn you had chosen. We used another one for the service. Our security film showed that Max's sister was looking into the urn before the service and later she asked me if she could have some of the ashes. When I refused, I was afraid she would try to steal them, so I have them secured. They are here waiting for you to take them."

"Thank you so much," said Donna. "I appreciate all your caring."

Donna had placed an obituary in the local paper in North Carolina and in the New Jersey newspaper in the area in which he was known, only to learn a month later that his mother had taken out a full page obituary with an old picture of Max and his late first wife, Carol, writing "finally together again" and never mentioning his children or Donna, like none of them ever existed.

Donna numbly walked through the motions of her life for the next couple of months, resting, taking care of herself, Alex, and her mother, and trying to make sense of it all. One evening, after life had seemed to settle down, she, Alex, Carl, and Carl's new wife took a stroll down to the dock by the lake. A fountain in the center of the lake spouted water up and over, cascading it down in a circle high above the lake. The light from a full moon sparkled on the still, crystal clear lake. They sat for a while in the quiet, cool night air, listening to the frogs chirp out their love songs and watching and listening to the beavers slapping the water with their huge tails. Then she pulled Max's urn from the bag, held it briefly, said a small prayer, then removed the lid and scattered the urn's contents on a light breeze that was blowing across the lake. Donna was at peace. She knew that Max believed in God so she knew where he was right at that moment, and that he was at peace now, too, the peace that he could never achieve in his earthly life. Both of their trials were over and finally, Donna could move on.

# Chapter 20

Nuts and Bolts

Although women are far more likely to be victims of Intimate Partner Violence, the distinction is not exclusively theirs. Men are victims, too. The percentage may be even higher than that recorded because men are more reluctant to report their attacks. They can be embarrassed to be assaulted by a woman because men continue to be viewed as the stronger sex and don't want to admit what people may perceive to be a weakness. Men tend to be more violent than women, so women are more at risk for physical harm. Women use more emotional, verbal and non-verbal coercive measures than violence to gain control over a partner. When they do resort to physical methods, they may throw things at the man, spit, kick, or bite. They may control the finances without allowing him to know about them; threaten to turn the children against him; or threaten to slander him in public. They can also do damage to a man's personal belongings. If a man would call the police, the woman may turn the tables on him and blame him for the altercation. Due to the prevailing belief that men are the abusers, authorities might believe her over him. Despite the more plentiful support networks there are for women, there is help for men, but there are no shelters because the need for them has not been shown at this time. For a website dedicated to helping men, follow the endnote.[22] If you know a man who may be in this position, please encourage him to get help. There is nothing to be ashamed of.

Another sub-group that one may not think about when considering IPV is same-sex relationships. It may or may not surprise you to know that the incidence of IPV in same-sex couples is equal to or possibly even more than, in heterosexual relationships. This is felt to be due to the different stressors involved with the population of people. Sometimes people are still in the closet and fear that by reporting abuse their sexual preferences will be exposed. Again, as with heterosexual men, the numbers of cases may be higher because of the lack of reporting. According to a 2018 article in Frontiers in Psychology, up to one third of men and up to one half of women in same-sex relationships reported experiencing psychological abuse.[23]

A group that can be easily minimized when discussing this topic is teenagers and it's referred to as teen dating violence.[24] Generally, they are not married nor do they live together, so they cannot be considered domestic violence, which is why the current, more inclusive, designation of Intimate Partner Violence is more appropriate as it picks up this group of people as well. Research shows that 26 % of women and 15 % of men who have been victims of sexual, emotional, physical, or stalking abuse report it started before they were 18 years old, Donna falling into that category, as well.[25] Many years ago, I knew a young lady who was a junior in high school, and she was dating a boy who was a year younger. She talked to me about the way he hit her when he got mad. If memory serves, she even had some bruises. Because I was in a position of confidentiality with this girl, I felt I couldn't tell anyone. She had a good relationship with her mother, so that was comforting to me to know. I tried to explain to her that she needed to get out of that relationship and that abuse doesn't usually get better, but it can escalate. I encouraged her to talk with her mother about it. When we moved to NC, I lost track of her, but after a little cyber-sleuthing (my kids call it stalking), I saw where she was married and had a child but not with him. I don't know if she did ever marry him, but she is safe now, as far as I know, and that's what matters.

College is even more troubling. This is when young people are exerting their independence and leaving the parental nest. Statistics show that 57 % of college graduates who have experienced dating abuse state that it happened in college.[26] Date rape is a huge problem on campuses and is felt to be under-reported for several reasons. A girl may really care about this person and doesn't want to get him in trouble. A girl may not understand the definition or the different categories of sexual assault. She may think no one will believe her. She doesn't want to ruin the boy's reputation. This is just to name a few.

It's not impossible for an abuser to change his stripes, but it is very difficult, and addictive behavior makes it even harder. Bear this in mind when you are trying to make a decision whether to leave or not after multiple promises of change. We have already discussed how deeply imbedded childhood experiences can be and how DNA can even be altered by repeated exposure to unhealthy circumstances and possibly passed down through generations. When we look at our combinations of nature and nurture in this light, we should be able to see how change can be hard. Hard, but not impossible. Since addiction fuels the rage involved in domestic violence, that addiction must be resolved first, before any other behavioral changes can be made. It was also mentioned earlier about how a person needs to want to change before that change can be made. Going through the motions of therapy because a partner won't let an abuser back in the house unless he does so is wasted time and money if that person doesn't honestly and sincerely want to change. Change requires intensive and difficult therapy and a person must sincerely accept that challenge. Hard to do, but not impossible.

Many, if not most, abusers have narcissistic personalities, which makes this change challenging. Since they don't think they are doing anything wrong they don't feel that they have anything to change. First and foremost in any quest for change: knowing they need help. If that can't be accomplished, then the effort is futile. An article in *Psychology Today* has a wonderful discussion of things abusers can do to help themselves heal because theirs is an illness, too.[27]

Abusers don't usually experience feelings of guilt because in their perception, everyone else is to blame. We saw this with both Max and his mother, Irene. This is a huge part of change: they must be able to take responsibility for themselves when things go wrong for them. It's is very difficult for narcissists to do but it is an essential part of healing. Feeling guilt is painful for anyone, but if someone can learn to be able to feel and tolerate that pain, or any other pain they feel, they will have taken a big step. It's just a fact of life that someone will hurt us at times, but we all must learn to deal with that person rationally and not lash out defensively. That will shut down healthy communication in a heartbeat. We must all allow ourselves to feel pain and deal with it in a healthy, non-abusive way.

Along these same lines of not believing they do anything wrong is a lack of understanding of what constitutes wrong and right. It could be that they think if they don't physically injure their partner, it's not abusive. They don't understand the concept of verbal insults as abuse. Some don't believe that stalking is abusive. That line might get a little blurry sometimes in some people's minds, but any unwanted action towards a partner is abuse, plain and simple. People need to be trained on the definition of abuse if they are unclear on it, and after they are trained, they need to accept it as truth.

Anger is a major emotion in IPV but is not usually the only one. Sometimes anger is just a smokescreen for underlying pain, sadness and insecurity. As we mentioned earlier, abusers sometimes can't feel guilt or pain, and so these feelings are pushed back down into the stovepipe and spill out the top in the form of anger. If a person is willing to work at separating these feelings and allowing them to come to the surface to be identified and dealt with, they will have a much better chance at getting the anger under control, and that's a big step.

One thing Donna said about Max is that he was "never humble," another manifestation of narcissism. If a person can do the other things like allowing themselves to feel pain, accepting responsibility for their actions, and learning to control anger, humility should, hopefully, follow. One can't be humble if he continues to place himself above everyone else.

Max had no empathy for others. He had occasional bursts of awareness of what he was doing to Donna, but they never lasted long. Understanding each other's reactions to situations and behaviors is essential to any relationship. Each one must try to be able to interpret what the other's actions might mean. It could be that her cold reactions have been programmed into her because of an abuser's treatment of her, but unless he can understand all the things mentioned above, he will not be able to feel empathy. He must learn to be open to understanding the why's. See how all these approaches work together towards a common goal?

That goal is change, but it cannot be accomplished alone. Abusive behavior was not formed overnight, just as victimhood was not formed overnight. They will not go away overnight. It takes commitment and accountability to create lasting positive changes in a person. Think about Weight Watchers as an example. People are more willing to try harder to control their diet if they know someone is monitoring them. AA operates on the same principle by assigning a mentor to new members. That's accountability. For those trying to effect change in behavior, a professional counselor is the person to hold them accountable. Abusers need to accept that this is not an easy or rapid process. There will be hills and valleys and they will need to develop patience when things aren't going well. They will have to learn to accept that, even if they change, the damage to their relationships may be irreversible and they may need to chalk it up to their own mistakes and vow not to make the same ones again. If a partner does choose to bring an abuser back into her life, he must be aware that trust doesn't form overnight, and it may be a long time before he can prove himself truly capable of change.

These are undeniably lofty goals for anyone to reach once destructive patterns of behavior have been formed, which is why the recidivism rate is still high among offenders, more so with violent offenders. There is a new approach being tried called "restorative justice". It involves bringing offenders and victims together in the same room with a mediator to discuss the social ramifications of the offenders actions. This novel approach is designed to make abusers aware of the harm their actions have caused and make them hold themselves accountable for it. The process is still in the early stages of development but is showing promise to reduce the recidivism rate among perpetrators of Intimate Partner Violence.

# Chapter 21

Let's Get Help

Abuse may stop, either by escape or by death, either the victim's or the abuser's, as it was with Max, but its effects may never truly disappear. It leaves permanent scars, physical and/or emotional, and survivors are charged with learning to deal with the fallout of that abuse.

I asked Donna what she thought would have happened if Max hadn't gotten sick. She thought about it a minute and said that she didn't think he would ever change, and she couldn't see any way of getting out. Unfortunately, this is a common problem. The volume of statistics and information on Intimate Partner Violence will make your head spin, but I was unable to find any on how many women ultimately get away from their abusers alive. What I did find, however, is that on average, a woman tries to leave her abuser seven times before she finally makes it out. Suffice to say that Donna is not alone. It's hard, and may I reiterate that women who choose to stay should not be judged. It's a complex problem and no one knows what they would do unless they had been in that situation themselves. Certainly, no one would wish that on anybody.

Donna's story and the information that was used to try and help you understand the dynamics of abuse is the tip of the iceberg. I tried to consolidate the information to what was more common and more significant, but there is so much more to know. The bright side is that help is available. As they say, an ounce of prevention is worth a pound of cure. If you are in a situation where you could possibly marry someone who abuses you or you see signs of an imminent problem, call it off and make him get treatment before you commit to a lifetime of pain, then make him prove he has changed by being consistent for a long time before you walk down the aisle. What's a long time? I think that is a question with many answers based on many factors. Let a professional help you decide. Remember that substance abuse is large piece of IPV because it's harder for an impaired person to control angry or violent impulses, so besides mental health counseling, he may need AA and/or Al-Anon. Abusers weave a tangled web.

There are some things you can do to help yourself if you are in a dangerous domestic situation:

1. Develop a strong support system. Utilize friends, family, or a spiritual leader for listening ears, but unless they are professional mental health care providers, they probably can't give you the proper tools to help you get out of a situation. The very best advice anyone would have to offer to you is to find a professional counselor, preferably one who is very familiar with intimate partner

violence. I understand this care can be costly, and often women in these situations cannot afford it or can't go without their partner providing the funds. Every municipality has a Department of Social Services who can help. Keep a list of numbers with you in the event of a crisis: the Crisis Hotline number, an emergency police number if you don't have 911 or a similar number in your area, your counselor's phone number, trusted friends who could pick you up in a hurry, a domestic violence shelter, and a taxi cab number, to name a few. If possible, memorize them. You may have others you want to add. One caveat to that, you must consider the safety of whoever is helping you, too, because 20 % of victims of domestic violence are not the partners but people trying to help them, like friends, family members, or police.[28]

2. Have an escape plan, but just like everything else in life, "safety first."[29] Know your partner's trigger points, the things that can set him off, and try to avoid them. Keep your eyes and ears open. If you sense a confrontation may be coming, find a logical reason for you and your children to leave the house. Thinking about some ahead of time will make it easier to do when it becomes necessary. If an outburst occurs and you can't get out, find a safe place in the house for you to go, again, plan for this ahead of time. Avoid closed rooms without an exit and anywhere that weapons may be kept, like the kitchen. Try to plan on getting to rooms that have a door or windows. It may not even be a bad idea to invest in a collapsible ladder to keep under a bed or in a closet. They are sold for use in fires, so that is a perfect reason for you to have them. Try to keep

your cell phone with you or head for a safe room that also has a land line. Establish a code word that you can share with your children, family, friends, neighbors, and co-workers to let them know you are in trouble and they should call the police.

3. Remember the Girl Scout motto, "Be Prepared." Make sure your car has enough fuel for you to get away in a hurry and that you have a spare key hidden. Find a box that you can hide where you can keep cash, clothing, a copy of the list of phone numbers you made and any important documents, preferably at a friend's house. If your children know what is happening in their home, which it's likely they do, share an escape plan with them and practice it when you are alone, just as you would a fire drill.

4. If you are unable to get out of the relationship at that time, there are a few things you can do to help. First, be in contact with the local domestic violence shelter so you will become familiar with where it is and what it is that they do. Try not to let him isolate you. You may be depressed and not want to socialize or even go anywhere but try to be involved in as many activities as you can safely do without causing a problem at home. Kid's activities, church activities, classes like exercise, dance or yoga are all excellent ways to keep physically and emotionally healthy, get out of the house, and establish a network of friends and other contacts for yourself. It may even be good, if you are financially able, to take some courses at a community college to either brush up on an old career or start a new one to prepare for a chance at financial independence. At least as important, if not more important, than all

those things, is building up your confidence and self-esteem. Identify things you are good at, or used to be good at, before someone told you that you weren't, and tune them up. Find things that will make you feel good about yourself again. Remember, we all have flaws, but we all are good at things, too. What did you like to do? Sing? Join a choir or a local vocal group. Dance? They have dance classes for all ages and abilities. Does it make you feel good to help people? Be a volunteer somewhere. Interestingly, Donna volunteered at a local shelter for women during her chaos, and it helped her cope with things at home. Avoid negative people. Surround yourself with positive thinking people who can build your mood up instead of knocking it down.

5. Protect your privacy. Keep your cell phone locked and install whatever apps you need to prevent your partner from having access to anything. Do the same thing with your computer. Use a neighbor's phone to call. Purchase a burner phone that you can keep in the secure escape box in case he destroys yours. If you have a GPS that can find your car, disable it. If you remember, Max had their house bugged. Be on the lookout for possible hidden cameras, like a Nanny Cam or even a baby monitor that can monitor your activities. Familiarize yourself with types of bugging devices and be alert for them. If you do find these things, don't disable them because it will alert your partner that you know about them. Just be aware that you are being monitored and act and speak accordingly without arousing suspicion. Hide books like these and any other literature that would suggest to him that you are planning a change.

6. If you are successful in leaving, take steps to protect yourself. Shelters are supposed to be anonymous, but, of course, they're not without risk. Change your usual routines. Go different routes to get to where you need to be. Be on constant alert to see if you are being followed, either by him or by a strange car that you see behind you repeatedly. Change your phone number or buy a new phone and change all your passwords. Take out a restraining order. You are already aware that these don't always work, but they're the best thing law enforcement has to offer. Help them help you. Don't allow yourself to be talked into breaking the order yourself. If you are seen doing this, you will lose your credibility as someone who is serious about her safety. As you know, abusers can charm the skin off a snake. Don't lose yours to the charm. File charges if he hurts you but make sure you have your safety plan set up first, because he's not going to be happy sitting in that jail cell. Be strong, because you are! Establish a relationship with a mental health provider and continue going after you are out of danger.

7. Be patient. Your fractured emotional state did not happen overnight, and it won't be cured overnight.

8. And last but certainly not least, is call the Domestic Violence Hotline number if you are in danger, or just to establish a relationship with them. They will direct you to a local shelter if you need to remove yourself from your current situation. *You can do this!*

*1-800-799-7233   TTY 1-800-787-3224*[30]

# Epilogue

I debated on whether I would disclose this next fact or not, but in order to accentuate the length and depth of pain domestic violence inflicts on a person's soul, and in the name of serendipity, or providence, if you prefer, I will tell you. I am "Anne," Max's hospice nurse. As I had mentioned earlier, I was also once a SANE or Sexual Assault Nurse Examiner. Because of this experience, I became more keenly aware of this very disturbing drag on society. Not too long ago I wrote a series of articles on these topics for my blog and Donna contacted me, asking me to tell her story. She had not recognized my name, but I knew hers immediately. Once I told her who I was, she remembered me, and we mutually felt that this project was meant to be. I am a children's book writer and had never written a full length book of any kind, but Donna wanted her story told, and we both wanted her message to be shared to help others who may be going through similar situations.

Max died thirteen years ago, and Donna has been carrying the weight of that abuse ever since then, and probably always will. She had tried several times to write her own story but was unsuccessful, both from an organizational and an emotional standpoint, Clearly, she never let the idea die. Donna's story ended safely for her, but it wouldn't be an acceptable ending for all survivors. It was difficult for her to separate which feeling she was having at any given time. She felt guilt, relief, regret, and sadness, all of which are totally normal responses to a loss such as hers.

At the time of this writing, Donna is retired and living in the same area of North Carolina but in a smaller, well-appointed home in a nice suburban neighborhood. Her penchant for décor is evident in this beautiful home. Her mother, Gina, is in her 90's and still manages to get around a little but her health is declining and Donna cares for her in her home, while still suffering from Lupus, herself. She is devoted to her mother. Donna has a fiancé who does have an anger issue, but he doesn't hit her. She no longer tolerates the nonsense, and he is learning to respect her for that. It seems those deep-seated childhood memories are still a part of her decision-making process in men, but she is now at least able to recognize that and stand up for herself. She still enjoys her iced mocha latte from the local coffee shop. Donna's sister, Julianna, got remarried and divorced again. She has a grown son and daughter and lives alone. Donna's boys all struggled with mental health issues and or substance abuse over the years, but all now are either married, engaged, or independent and seem to be doing alright. They are also survivors. She has not seen her first son, Ronnie, since the incident at his mother's funeral. He has distanced himself from everyone except his adopted father. Donna does keep in touch with her daughter-in-law and grandchildren from Ronnie.

Max's mother and father are both still alive but getting on in years. Danny and the rest of Max's siblings are still alive, also, but the feud with Max's family continues and Donna does not see or talk to any of them.

Although Donna's freedom was delivered to her upon her abuser's death, she did survive his abuse, and you can, too. It is possible to get out of an abusive situation, even if you live in the prettiest house in the neighborhood. It's not easy, but entirely possible. Get help. Believe in yourself. You are strong, and you got this!

# ABOUT THE AUTHOR

Pat was born in sunny Florida but lived there for only 10 weeks when she, her older sister, and her mom moved up north to Bethlehem, Pennsylvania to live with her grandparents. She graduated from Liberty High School and St. Luke's Hospital School of Nursing in Bethlehem, and thereafter enjoyed a long career in nursing. Her husband and three children moved from Pennsylvania to North Carolina in 1990, and her fourth child was born in Durham, NC, the only natural born Tar Heel in the family. Her mother never had any secondary education, but she had a love of writing that she instilled in Pat. While working as a nurse and raising her family, Pat wrote for fun, for expressing her opinions in newspapers, and as a creative outlet for herself. It wasn't until she retired from nursing that she actively pursued her dream of becoming a serious writer. She, like her mother, had no formal education in the literary arts, but learned on her own, using her passion as a guide to create. Since retiring, she has written two children's books prior to *The Prettiest House on the Block*. *The Giggle Box* was inspired by her children, and *The Town of Alpaca* was inspired by visiting an alpaca farm in the Blue Ridge Mountains of Virginia. This book went on to win third place in the CIPA (Colorado Independent Publishers Association) EVVY awards in the Children's Fictional Storybook category in 2019. Besides her love of writing and love for her family, Pat readily shares her faith in God. She also loves her big, furry dog, Dakota, a Native American Shepherd, and she enjoys sewing and gardening. She has five wonderful grandchildren to date, all of whom, along with her children and husband, Denny, are lights in her life. You can learn more by visiting her websites at
https://wordpress.com/view/patricschrn.wordpress.com and
https://www.facebook.com/PatSchochAuthor/

# Endnotes

[1] https://www.cdc.gov/violenceprevention/intimatepartnerviolence/index.html

[2] https://www.helpguide.org/articles/grief/coping-with-grief-and-loss.htm

[3] https://psmag.com/social-justice/childhood-trauma-adversely-affects-decision-making

[4] https://psmag.com/social-justice/childhood-trauma-adversely-affects-decision-making

[5] https://psmag.com/social-justice/childhood-trauma-adversely-affects-decision-making

[6] https://www.simplypsychology.org/maslow.html

[7] https://www.mayoclinic.org/diseases-conditions/primary-immunodeficiency/symptoms-causes/syc-20376905

[8] https://www.theatlantic.com/family/archive/2019/05/divorced-parents-marriage/590425/

[9] https://www.refinery29.com/en-gb/domestic-abuse-rehabilitation

[10] https://www.domesticshelters.org/articles/faq/domestic-violence-statistics

[11] https://www.newsobserver.com/news/local/crime/article237578909.html

[12] https://www.newsob server.com/news/local/crime/article237578909.html

[13] https://geneticliteracyproject.org/2014/10/29/genes-linked-to-violent-crime-but-can-they-

explain-criminal-behavior/

[14] https://geneticliteracyproject.org/2014/10/29/genes-linked-to-violent-crime-but-can-they-explain-criminal-behavior/

[15] https://www.discovermagazine.com/health/can-we-blame-our-genes-for-our-decisions

[16] https://apnews.com/d623151897214fe1871c96a47cf3d7cc

[17] https://www.psychologytoday.com/us/basics/fantasies

[18] https://www.psychologytoday.com/us/conditions/narcissistic-personality-disorder

[19] https://www.drugabuse.gov/publications/drugfacts/genetics-epigenetics-addiction

[20] https://www.drugabuse.gov/publications/drugfacts/genetics-epigenetics-addiction

[21] https://www.drugabuse.gov/publications/drugfacts/genetics-epigenetics-addiction

[22] https://www.thehotline.org/2014/07/22/men-can-be-victims-of-abuse-too/

[23] https://www.ncbi.nlm.nih.gov/pmc/articles/PMC6113571/

[24] https://www.cdc.gov/violenceprevention/intimatepartnerviolence/teendatingviolence/fastfact.html

[25] https://www.cdc.gov/violenceprevention/intimatepartnerviolence/teendatingviolence/fastfact.html

[26] https://www.cdc.gov/violenceprevention/intimatepartnerviolence/teendatingviolence/fastfact.html

[27] https://www.psychologytoday.com/us/blog/hurt-people-hurt-people/201511/abusive-partners-can-change

[28] https://ncadv.org/statistics

[29] https://www.helpguide.org/articles/abuse/getting-out-of-an-abusive-relationship.htm

[30] https://www.thehotline.org/help/

Made in the USA
Middletown, DE
07 September 2020